A Special Collection from The Journal of Commercial Bank Lending

CREDIT ANALYSIS

rma ROBERT MORRIS ASSOCIATES
The National Association of Bank Loan and Credit Officers
Philadelphia, Pennsylvania

About Robert Morris Associates

Robert Morris Associates (RMA) is the national association of bank loan and credit officers. Founded in 1914, RMA has grown to more than 3,000 commercial banks and thrift institutions, which account for 85% of the C & I lending done by these types of U.S. financial institutions. These institutions are represented in the association by more than 13,000 commercial loan and credit officers and related personnel in all 50 states, Puerto Rico, Canada, and several offshore cities.

RMA was named after the American patriot who signed the Declaration of Independence, was largely responsible for the financing of our Revolutionary War, and helped establish our banking system.

The association's original purpose back in 1914 was to facilitate the flow and interchange of credit information. Today, this purpose has been expanded to include working continuously to improve the principles and practices of commercial lending, loan administration, and asset management in commercial banks.

RMA seeks to fulfill its purpose by providing commercial bankers with programs, products, and services they need to increase their proficiency in lending, credit, and related areas. RMA's reason for being, then, is to provide these bankers with the tools they need to make better loans, keep abreast of the continual changes that affect the lending function, and, at the bottom line, help them increase the profitability of their institutions.

Library of Congress Catalog Card Number: 86-28628
International Standard Book Number: 0-936742-38-0

Library of Congress Cataloging in Publication Data

Credit analysis.

Contents: Credit analysis, tying it all together, part I; Credit analysis, tying it all together, part II / Dennis C. Eisenreich—A philosophical foundation for credit analysis / David B. Still—Working capital theory revisited / Jeffrey W. Miller—[etc.]
1. Credit—Management. 2. Bank loans. 3. Cash flow. I. Robert Morris Associates. II. Journal of commercial bank lending.

HG1641.C66 1987 332.1'753'0685 86-28628
ISBN 0-936742-38-0

Additional copies of this publication are available from the Order Department, Robert Morris Associates, 1616 Philadelphia National Bank Bldg., Philadelphia, PA 19107 (215) 665-2850.

Table of Contents

Introduction

For the nearly 70 years that *The Journal of Commercial Bank Lending* has been published, there have probably been more articles printed on some aspect of credit analysis than on any other single lending topic. Therefore, credit analysis was a logical choice of subject matter for this sixth special collection of articles from the *Journal*.*

However, selecting which articles to include in the collection was not an easy task. A study of recently published articles on the topic resulted in a list of 22 articles from which to choose. At that point, three experienced bankers, all specialists in credit administration, were asked to review the 22 articles and recommend those they considered best for the collection.

Using the reviewers' thoughtful evaluations, we decided that 12 articles merited inclusion in this book. These articles thus represent the highest quality discussions on credit analysis published in the *Journal* during the past seven years. And to ensure that these articles remain timely, the authors were given an opportunity to review and update their articles. Where authors had new observations to share, you will find an "Author's Update" at the end of the article.

The articles

The collection is divided into four sections, the first being "Credit Analysis: Overview and Important Issues." The articles in this section—a two-parter entitled, "Credit Analysis: Tying It All Together," by Dennis Eisenreich and "A Philosophical Foundation for Credit Analysis" by David B. Still—provide an excellent introduction to the topic of credit analysis.

The second section of the collection, "Working Capital and Cash Flow Analysis," looks at both working capital and cash flow as related concepts in credit analysis. The first article in this section, "Working Capital Theory Revisited" by Jeffrey W. Miller, is a true classic and views working capital in a way that all bankers will want to consider.

The next article in the second section, "Cash Flow—The Most Critical Issue of the 1980s" by James E. Perry, discusses the quality of working capital and timing differences and the impact on cash flows. Lyn M. Fraser's article, "Cash Flow from Operations and Liquidity Analysis: A New Financial Ratio

* The other five Special Collections from the *Journal* published thus far are *Loan Review* (December 1984), *Spilled Milk*—stories on loans that went sour (April 1985), *Problem Loans* (November 1985), *Risk Management* (February 1986), and *Real Estate and Construction Lending* (April 1986).

for Commercial Lending Decisions,'' follows Perry's and adds a new ratio to the discussion of working capital and cash flow. The information in the article is still timely, although it contains some sample financial statements dated as of the end of 1981 and 1982.

Another classic is ''Analyzing the Quantity and Quality of Cash Flow for Long-Term Borrowing'' by Dev Strischek. It is the fourth article in the working capital and cash flow section and covers basic cash flow concepts. In the last article in this section, ''The Recession-Sensitive Borrower: Evaluating Cash Flow and Financial Structure,'' John R. Carter uses three good examples to make his points concerning cash flow calculation. Although we are not currently in a recession, Carter's article contains much useful information, which will undoubtedly come in handy when the economy again takes a downturn.

The third section of the collection, ''Financial Statement Analysis,'' presents two fine articles that are closely related: ''Examining Personal Financial Statements'' by Christopher Volk and ''Using Tax Returns as Credit Analysis Tools'' by Maurice F. Claeys. Much of what is emphasized in the latter article is often overlooked by credit analysts.

''Break-Even Analysis'' is the title of the last section, which contains these two articles: ''Break-Even Analysis and Operating Leverage'' by Dev Strischek and ''More on Break-Even Analysis'' by Venkatesan Srinivasan. Borrowers need to know what their break-even point is, and these two articles will tell them and their bankers how to determine that point.

Acknowledgments

I would like to thank the three hard-working reviewers who provided their invaluable assistance and expertise to this Special Collection on credit analysis. They are Joan P. Hofmann, formerly a vice president, credit policy-training, Crocker National Bank, San Francisco; J. Kempton Shields, senior vice president, Sovran Bank, N.A., Richmond, Va.; and Charles J. Wolf, vice president, United Missouri Bank of Kansas City, N.A.

All three reviewers have been active in National RMA's Credit Division. Hofmann was a member of the Credit Division Council, Shields has been a Fall Conference speaker and instructor in national Credit Division workshops, and Wolf is serving as chairman of the Statement Studies Committee for the second year. The work of these reviewers and, of course, the contributions made by the ten authors whose articles appear here have been essential to the completion of this special collection.

Charlotte Weisman, Editor
The Journal of Commercial Bank Lending
Robert Morris Associates
Philadelphia, Pennsylvania

Credit Analysis: Overview and Important Issues

Credit Analysis: Tying It All Together—Part I

by Dennis C. Eisenreich

The following is the first part of a two-part article on credit analysis that places more emphasis on the need for sound judgment than on technical skills. Among the topics discussed in Part I are the judgment of credit risk, the consideration of human variables, and the interpretation of economic variables. Part II is the article immediately following.

The author is vice president and manager, Small Business Division, Mellon Bank, N.A., Pittsburgh, Pennsylvania. At the time this article was first published in December 1981, Mr. Eisenreich was a vice president at Mellon.

Successful commercial lending requires judgment more than it requires technical skills. An understanding of accounting, financial analysis, and various types of loans may help a lender ask the "right" questions. But the critical issues must be judged from the numerous variables under consideration. Judgment may also be required to verify those critical issues with objective sources.

Judging credit risk

Since repayment always occurs in the future, the lender must judge whether the borrower's expectations about the capacity to repay are reasonable. If he judges that they are not, the lender must then assess the capacity to repay from alternative sources. If the lender becomes confident of repayment, the appropriate type of financing must be fit to the circumstances in order to have the payment record help the lender monitor the loan's progress. Throughout the process, the lender's technical skills may be invaluable in asking the right questions. However, determining whether the answers are "reasonable" requires judgment, often conditioned with time and experience.

The purpose of credit analysis

While credit analysis must always be directed at the capacity to repay, what is it that a lender is trying to identify in the financial statements and other information that may have been gathered? Unless that is clear, the lender may waste a great deal of valuable time, not to mention the consequences of reaching the wrong decision. Thus, any discussion of credit analysis must begin with some definitions of credit risk. The ultimate risk characteristics may be either:

- The *inability* of cash inflows to meet necessary cash outflows (so-called "cash insolvency") or
- The *inability* of cash inflows to meet necessary cash outflows *on schedule* (referred to as "cash inadequacy").

While the consequences of cash insolvency for the bank would typically be a loss, cash inadequacy may simply mean slow payment. Unfortunately, the inability to pay the bank on time probably implies things have not gone as expected. To fully pay the bank, management may have to make decisions (for example, an unusual asset liquidation) that would otherwise be undesirable for the firm, the owners, and possibly other creditors. Since it is never clear what management might do under these conditions, cash inadequacy may quickly lead to cash insolvency and a loss.

Since banks are theoretically in the business of taking risk, why are lenders so concerned about losses? All lenders should have a clear understanding of the basis for such concern. Although the rate may be raised with the probability of loss for a given loan, an individual loan cannot be priced for a loss. For example, if the bank's net interest margin (that is, interest income less interest expense over average assets) is equal to 4% for a year, it would take 25 years to cover the loss of 100% of principal, not to mention related overhead costs. With a clear understanding of the fact that banks *cannot* lose much on average, the initial response may be to avoid lending. Loan income is, however, required to cover costs and show any earnings for the bank. Therefore, lenders must make loans without losing very much. Herein lies the dilemma that can only be solved with careful credit analysis and sound credit judgment.

Credit judgment

Figure 1 outlines a decision-making process for systematically formulating and updating a credit judgment. Along the left side, the more extensive process associated with a totally new credit is broadly outlined. On the right side, the process of updating a judgment for existing customers is covered. Both sides are directed at the fundamental principle of evaluating the risk of not getting paid on schedule. Too often with prospects representing significant relationship

Figure 1—Outlining the Process of Forming/Updating Credit Judgments

Formulating Credit Judgments for Prospects	Updating Credit Judgments for Existing Customers
1. Acquire Basic Information about Borrower	
A. Historical and Current Financial Statements B. Background Information	A. Current Financial Statements B. Broad Explanation of Current Performance
2. Acquire Basic Information about Loans	
A. Size and Purpose of Proposed Needs B. Sources of Repayment	A. Size and Purpose of New Loans B. Status and Use of Existing Loans C. Sources of Repayment D. Condition/Value of Collateral (If Any)
3. Preliminary Review of Risk (including identification of need for more information or clarification)	
A. Assess Commitment, Experience, and Track Record of Human Variables B. Assess Broad Political and Economic Risks C. Identify Operating Strengths and Weaknesses Apparent in Track Record D. Evaluate Strength and Stability of Cash Flow in Relation to Historical Demands E. Anticipate Future Operating Performance and Investment Needs (Considering Proposed Loan) and Capacity to Service Debt F. Evaluate Balance Sheet Strengths and Weaknesses and Consequences of Loan G. Determine Superficial Risk Rating to Guide the Rest of the Process	A. Evaluate Change or Inconsistencies in Human Variables B. Reevaluate Changing Political or Economic Risks C. Evaluate Current Operating Performance Against Expectations D. Evaluate Recent Cash Flow and Investment Decisions in Relation to Plans and Financial Consequences E. Anticipate Future Operating Performance and Investment Needs (Considering Proposed Loan) and Capacity to Service Debt F. Evaluate Balance Sheet Strengths and Weaknesses and Consequences of Loan G. Evaluate Loan Covenants and Supplementary Information H. Determine Any Likely Change in Existing Risk Rating

Figure 1, continued

4. Acquire More Complete Information

A. Details of Proposed Deal
B. Details of Important Human Considerations
C. Details of Important Operating Considerations
D. General Financial Objectives and Plans
E. Supplemental Financial Information (such as Projections)

A. Details of Proposed Deal
B. Explanation of Changes in Human Variables
C. Explanations of Significant Operating Issues or Problems
D. Expectations of Significant Investments or Problems Requiring Financing
E. Supplemental Financial Information (such as Projections)

5. Verify Critical Information

A. On-site Visits
B. Routine Bank, Trade, and Possibly Customer Checks
C. Routine Trade Information
D. Broad Industry Checks (Public Sources or Direct Investigation)
E. Require Audited Statements

A. On-site Visits
B. Specific Investigation
C. Routine Trade Information
D. Check Industry Problems/ Outlook
E. Dispatch Collateral Auditors

6. Refined Analysis of Risk

A. Establish Commitment of Owners and Labor
B. Assess Management's Success and Determination to Pay Loans
C. Judge Political and Economic Risk for Future
D. Identify and Weigh Operating Strengths and Weaknesses
E. Evaluate Expectations for Operating Performance (Considering Proposed Loan)
F. Evaluate, Project, and Estimate Strength of Cash Flow in Relation to All Demands (including Proposed Debt Service)
G. Estimate Current or Potential Pressures on Working Capital
H. Evaluate Secondary Protection of Balance Sheet, Collateral, or Guarantees

A. Reassess Commitment
B. Assess Recent Human Decision Making
C. Interpret Changes in Political and Economic Risks
D. Identify and Weigh Operating Strengths and Weaknesses
E. Evaluate Expectations for Operating Performance (Considering Proposed Loan)
F. Evaluate, Project, and Estimate Strength of Cash Flow in Relation to All Demands (including Proposed Debt Service)
G. Estimate Current or Potential Pressures on Working Capital
H. Evaluate Secondary Protection of Balance Sheet, Collateral, or Guarantees

Figure 1, continued

7. Make Overall Decision

A. Assign an Overall Risk Rating (Formally or Informally) B. If Rating Is Unacceptable, the Process Ends	A. Keep or Change Existing Risk Rating B. If Rating Becomes Unacceptable, Collection Must be Assessed and a Plan Proposed

8. Structure Loan

A. Determine Appropriate Type, Maturity, and Pricing to Fit Needs and Risk B. If Terms Required Are Unacceptable able, the Process Ends C. Seek Appropriate Approvals D. Negotiate Acceptable Terms E. Document and Close Loan	A. For New Loans, Determine Appropriate Type, Maturity, and Pricing to Fit Needs and Risk B. If Terms Are Unacceptable the Project May Need to be Reconsidered C. Seek Appropriate Approvals D. Negotiate Acceptable Terms E. Restructure Deal to Meet Changing Needs for Existing Loans F. Review Problem Loans with Appropriate Collection Area G. Document and Close New Loans

---

potential, busy lenders assume the capacity to repay and move on to pricing considerations far too early. However, lenders considering existing customers whose circumstances are deteriorating probably have the most difficulty, at least initially, in clearly evaluating the growing risks of not getting paid. As a result, the basic elements of formulating or updating a credit decision are the same.

While Figure 1 is only one individual's version of the decision-making process, several elements are fundamental. Foremost is the "Catch-22" of bank lending. To determine risk requires "complete" information. But to know what "complete" information means for a given credit requires a determination of risk. Since no standard amount of information will necessarily be complete, the basic information gathered about the borrower and proposed loan will be used to formulate a preliminary judgment. Of course, such a judgment is made carefully since the information is potentially incomplete and typically unsubstantiated. If the risk is judged to be minimal or normal, the next step may be principally for clarification and verification. If the risk is judged to be above normal, a great deal of additional information may be required to assess the risk properly. Otherwise, credits that may be more unusual than risky would be rejected and potentially good customers lost. At any rate, the preliminary judgment guides the nature and depth of the subsequent analysis.

Acquiring more complete information from a borrower is a logical part of the process, *not* something the lender should be timid about. Another *critical* aspect is the verification of important information. Typical forms of verification include audited statements (as the credit rises and especially for unsecured loans), direct investigations (with suppliers, customers, and possibly competitors), and on-site visits. With on-site visits, lenders should:

1. Anticipate what they expect to see.

2. Try to understand how the business works generally.

3. Ask about things they do not understand (especially as they relate to profitable operations and asset/collateral values).

If management's explanations and expectations correspond to credible industry sources, such information may be considered to some extent verified.

After doing a refined analysis of the facts, the difficult step of judging the risk must be taken. Figure 1 suggests assigning a credit risk rating. While some lenders fight the very notion of rating credits, most of those same lenders have no difficulty identifying the above average, average, and below average credits in their loan portfolios. One may suspect risk ratings have been the best kept secrets of good lenders for a very long time. Of course, to assign a rating, the lender must assign weights of importance to the facts that may be, by themselves, both positive and negative. Choosing what is and is not potentially significant is *the* critical part of a credit judgment.

With the overall decision on the credit risk, the process will either end (if the risk is too great) or move to the structure of the loan. Before leaving this issue, some discussion of risk ratings is in order. Good credit risks are not necessarily good customers. The best customers (in terms of profitability and loyalty) tend to be average or slightly below average credits. While Figure 1 ends with the closing of an appropriately structured and priced loan for prospects, it should be clear that the prospect then becomes an existing customer. As such, the judgment must be periodically updated.

Subsequent sections discuss some of the traditional elements of risk (that is, human, economic, and financial elements). Each must be understood individually before it can be properly evaluated within the overall context of the credit. Considering the ultimate task is to weight various factors in arriving at a credit judgment, the lender must appreciate the importance of individual issues.

Considering human variables

Human decisions can have some of the most profound and unpredictable consequences for a firm. For this reason, human considerations must take a priority position in all credit judgments. Such human variables usually involve owners, managers, and labor.

Potential consequences of concentrated ownership

The first human consideration is always an understanding of the principal owners. A clear identification of owners and affiliated companies is critical to any expectations about the future of the firm under consideration. If the owner has a heavy debt burden to meet and few alternative sources of income, is it reasonable to expect dividends to be restricted? If the firm under consideration is supplied by or sells to an affiliate company at something other than market prices, how valuable is historical operating performance in projecting future profitability? In other words, a modest dividend in the past and a profitable track record as a result of significant sales to an affiliate with a marginal performance record are not necessarily good indicators of the future.

The potential for unpredictable decisions by ownership concentrated in a few hands may reduce the value of the track record as an indicator. To the extent professional managers run the firm, owners may actually replace management which may completely reduce the value of the track record. Concentrated ownership may also represent a strength. Owners of proprietorships or general partnerships may directly contribute significant alternative strength. Corporate owners through guarantees may also offer substantial alternative strength. If lenders must rely on the certainty of such secondary protection, the owner's worth should exclude the investment in the borrowing firm and any other assets (for example, loans and single-purpose buildings) used in the firm to clearly identify alternative strength and to avoid double counting the circumstances of the borrowing firm.

Management: the "intangible" variable

Although a great deal is written about the management factor, the consideration can be reduced to (1) the evaluation of management's success and (2) the estimate of management's determination to repay. In evaluating management's ongoing success, the clearest evidence is successful and related experience through good and bad times. Future success may depend on an active role for successor managers. As the business grows or changes, additional skills (particularly, financial) must be developed or bought.

The more difficult issue to evaluate is management's determination to repay. Words like *character, willingness,* and *integrity* are commonly used to describe this issue. But if management has a clear determination to pay, any circumstances that lead to cash inadequacy will probably not lead to serious collection problems. A determination to pay can easily be portrayed in what a management says, but it can only be reliably established in what a management does. Thus, actions taken to reduce debt during difficult times in the past (possibly, during the recession) represent concrete evidence. Conservative financial managers always illustrate a determination to repay. More aggressive managers may show the determination to repay through realistic financial planning (such as through projections) that has been reliable in the past. Of course, the lender must also respect the customer's integrity or honesty. Since the majority of information will come from the borrower, as discussed under the section on credit judgment, the lender must have confidence in the raw material of the judgment. If not or if critical facts cannot be verified, the lender cannot make the decision. It would be a gamble rather than a calculated risk.

Labor

The attitude of labor can make or break most firms. As the required level of skill increases, labor can represent a severely limiting factor. Although contract negotiations with unions may represent temporary disruptions that are more serious for some firms than others, chronic and unpredictable wildcat strikes probably cause more problems. The productivity of labor compared to competitors is often the principal explanation of comparatively low profits or losses. It is neither an easy variable to identify nor an easy problem to solve.

Interpreting economic variables

Assuming reasonable human decisions, much of the risk is essentially related to the economic environment. Measuring the economic considerations must begin with distinctions made between economic levels. The diagram in Figure 2 suggests a method of categorizing economic levels.

Figure 2—Economic Levels

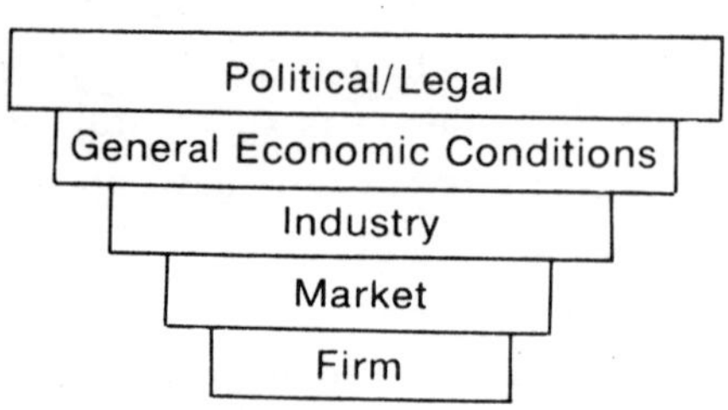

Before a lender can successfully deal with economic analysis at the firm level, some understanding of the other levels is required. The other levels may introduce risk or uncertainty that is beyond the control of managers.

Market: where the competition is

Most firms operate on a regional or local level. The market represents the demand for their products or services in a reasonably defined geographic market. Understanding the existing and potential markets of firms will help in identifying who their customers are and who their competitors are. The diagram in Figure 3 identifies some of the basic considerations.

Figure 3—Market Variables

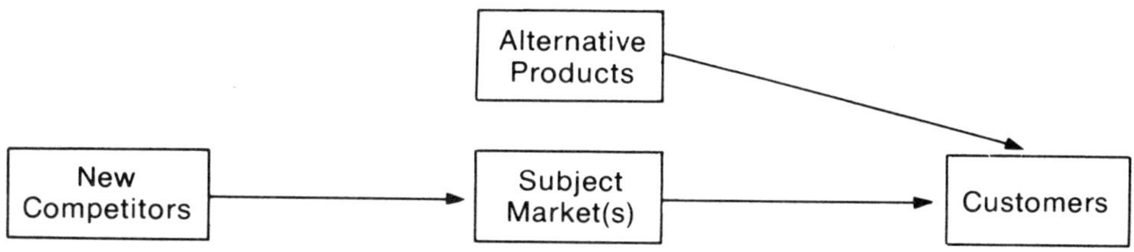

The track record performance can be transformed by new competitors and alternative products that serve the same need. Existing competition may become more pronounced as the growth in the underlying customer base slows. Market considerations dominate the evaluation of retailers and wholesalers because product lines can be altered. As a result, the location with respect to customers is always a critical consideration.

Industry: understanding the character of operations

The industry represents the *supply* of products that are close substitutes in satisfying the same needs. In order to identify anything that could affect a firm's operating costs, sales volumes, or prices (that is, business risks), some understanding of the industry is required. Lenders should take every opportunity to learn about their customers' business from all credible sources. Although no lender can be an expert in all industries to which a loan may be made, the lender can be sufficiently knowledgeable to ask questions and identify reasonable answers. After all, it requires far less to understand *how* something works than it does to make it work.

Many of the basic industry risks can be identified by the diagram in Figure 4.

Figure 4—Industry Variables

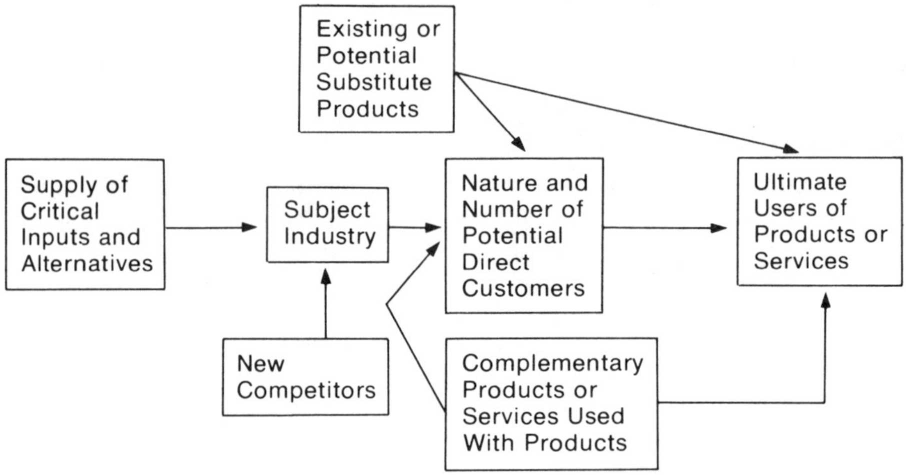

First, the borrower (particularly, an industrial firm) should be fit into the stages of production. Knowing what it buys, what it does with it, who it sells it to, and what must be used with it represents the obvious beginning. A plant visit and tour may give the banker an opportunity to understand the nature of the business, to view managers in their own element, and to demonstrate an interest.

Second, the characteristics of "ultimate" demand should be identified. In this process, cyclical and secular trends that could affect the level of future sales potential are considered. Typically, a clear understanding of the causes of past trends at the firm and industry levels helps to anticipate future trends. Of course, fundamental change in the industry or firm diversification may result in more or less volatile operating results in the future than indicated by the track record.

To understand the need, a lender may have to identify the borrower's customers (or possibly customers' customers). If that need is easily filled by others in the industry or by substitute products, competition may be based on price so cost advantages would be required. If the need requires a quality product or ongoing service, price may be less important than superior design features, durability, and service (with their associated costs). Such an understanding of the "nature of competition" will help the lender evaluate past and anticipate future operating results.

The third step includes the identification of substitutes, new competitors, or complements. Existing or potential substitutes represent alternatives for the firm's customers that can affect future sales levels and prices suddenly.

New competitors with significant financial, technical, or marketing advantages may dramatically change the rules of the game. If the cost of using a product rises because of the price of a product used with it (tires to gasoline), the firm's sales may be affected. Each of these circumstances can reduce the value of the track record in anticipating the future.

Finally, the ability to cover costs and ensure availability of critical inputs represents potential supply problems. The consequences of rapidly rising costs for a firm can be significant if other producers have more stable costs or the rising price makes a close substitute increasingly more attractive. In addition, a firm in a competitive industry that sells to relatively few customers may be forced to absorb part of the cost increases. As bad as rising costs are, the inability to access a critical input is worse. A product cannot be sold unless it can be finished. Thus, in addition to labor strikes and raw material shortages, transportation bottlenecks, pollution curtailments, natural gas shortages (without backup), and severe weather can all affect actual production.

The broad secular trend of an industry can probably be divided into developmental, growth, mature, and declining phases. The phase can affect opportunities for loans, potential for repayment, and analytical considerations.

In the developmental phase, the industry is characterized by (1) slow and uncertain sales growth and (2) unpredictable costs and asset values. Since both primary and secondary sources of repayment are at best uncertain, very good alternative protection would be required to meet the indicated borrowing need. In the growth phase, an obvious need for funds to support the growth in assets could possibly be justified with a track record demonstrating a capacity to generate cash over and above minimal requirements. In the mature phase, significant competition may result from individual firms attempting to maintain growth rates. If an industry appears to have reached a *long-term* declining phase, lenders should be particularly careful in considering term loan requests. Controlled short-term lending may continue to be reasonable.

General business conditions: interpreting the "big picture"

Since the bulk of published economic information concerns the economy, the lender must be able to interpret the implications of broad economic trends for individual borrowers. The logical connection is with the industry or the market. An industry may be cyclical if it manufactures a product or provides a service that is easily postponed by its customers (discretionary) or that is dependent on a broad level of business activity (such as industrial products and transportation services). Of course, not all industries are affected significantly by the business cycle. The general business conditions in a particular market can have disastrous results on firms locked into those markets. Such conditions may be related to (1) regional economic trends (general unemployment, personal income, and inflation) that gradually affect discretionary income or (2) specific regional events (closing of a significant employer and a flood) that suddenly affect numerous businesses.

Even firms insulated from significant economic shocks may have to bear a broad economic consequence through the bank. Banks that must raise interest rates in line with higher cost sources of purchased funds will force this economic condition onto their customers. Different firms will have more or less difficulty in covering interest. At the extreme, tight money may dramatically restrict a firm's potential. To anticipate rising interest rates, the borrower will always look to the banker for information on what to expect. Although predicting future interest rates is one part speculation and one part wild guess, lenders must help borrowers address this issue. A significant misjudgment of carrying costs in a new project can be the difference between accepting or rejecting a proposal.

Political framework: knowing the rules of the game

Beyond the impact government fiscal and monetary policies may have on general business conditions, the political framework has various effects on a firm. Government policies affect taxes and numerous costs such as environmental and health and safety expenditures. In regulated industries, government action affects prices and possibly volumes such as forced curtailments. The political framework may also affect the legal composition chosen by the borrower. Thus, lending to proprietorships, partnerships, or corporations requires different considerations. Borrowers who utilize numerous legal corporations introduce additional complications for the lender in having access to assets. Properly documenting the loan is a necessary skill for the lender to master.

The political framework is a particularly difficult part of the analysis to anticipate because it is subject to compromise decision making. Fortunately, most competitors will be equally affected by federal political decisions. To the extent local political decisions are involved (for example, state taxes or environmental requirements), firms may be put at a competitive disadvantage. Thus, lenders must factor political considerations into the lending decision. □

Credit Analysis: Tying It All Together—Part II

by Dennis C. Eisenreich

In Part II of his article on credit analysis, Dennis Eisenreich discusses the importance of working capital, short- and intermediate-term lending, and the various facets of financial analysis. Part I is the article immediately preceding.

The author is vice president and manager, Small Business Division, Mellon Bank, N.A., Pittsburgh, Pennsylvania. At the time this article was first published in January 1982, Mr. Eisenreich was a vice president at Mellon.

Much of the risk in commercial lending—the risk of not getting paid on schedule due to cash inadequacy—is related to human and economic variables. However, the clearest evidence of risk is related to financial variables.

Evaluating financial variables

To define financial variables, it may be easiest to consider cash inflows separately from cash outflows. Since the major cash inflows for any successful firm will depend on sales levels and prices, the ability to get enough sales at the right prices is a key element of the overall risk (often called *business risk*). Cash outflows typically result from necessary business activity such as the payment of wages and raw material purchases and financial decisions as reflected in, for example, capital expenditures and debt service. The need to meet these obligations is often referred to as *financial risk*.

To avoid cash inadequacy, expected cash inflows must be capable of meeting minimum cash outflows on schedule. As long as creditors and owners have confidence in this capacity over the long run, borrowings and possibly equity contributions will probably be available for temporary shortfalls or discretionary outflows such as conscious decisions to expand or add plant equipment.

Working capital: Why is it so important?

In an attempt to limit financial considerations to a manageable set, the financial element of risk is defined as the inability of cash generation to:

1. Maintain working capital.
2. Maintain productive assets.
3. Meet debt service on schedule.
4. Pay reasonable dividends.
5. Maintain some borrowing power.

Cash generation is defined as profits plus depreciation. Assuming the accountant's matching concept is working properly (one indication of the need to understand accounting), profits represent the portion of sales dollars that are otherwise uncommitted to period expenses.

Depreciation represents a return of previous cash investment that is often considered committed either to replacing fixed assets (that is, necessary capital expenditures) or to servicing debt originally used to purchase the property. Of course, *cash* generation (sometimes called *cash flow* or *cash throw-off*) is somewhat of a misnomer since the actual cash may remain tied up in uncollected sales (receivables) or be quickly reinvested in necessary inventories. Nevertheless, cash generation is the most reliable source of internal funds eventually available to meet various long-term demands. Because cash generation is important as an indicator of the future, it should always be adjusted for nonrecurring events, both positive and negative.

Any firm that does not show sufficient cash generation to cover these additional demands is already in a state of cash inadequacy. A temporary cash shortfall with little prospect for improvement can have serious consequences. Much of the subsequent financial analysis will be built around these demands on cash generation.

Of the alternative long-term demands on the cash generated, most lenders clearly acknowledge the maintenance of capital expenditures, the requirement of debt service, and dividend requirements. While excessive or unproductive capital expenditures may be restricted by a loan agreement, no lender would consciously restrict required capital expenditures. The consequence could be costly breakdowns.

Slow debt repayment may be the most current clue a banker has as to cash inadequacy. Naturally, all bankers follow past due principal and interest reports for this reason. In fact, by the time a borrower is forced to delay paying any debt, numerous payments, such as for trade debt, may already have been delayed.

Finally, a reasonable dividend payout is probably justified in all but high-risk situations. Most term loan covenants acknowledge this claim by restricting only a cumulative percentage of profits. Of course, all dividends may be restricted, but the lender may be giving concentrated owners an incentive to circumvent the agreement or to replace management.

The additional requirements for cash generation to satisfy minimum working capital requirements and to provide some borrowing power are less well understood. The borrowing power issue will subsequently be discussed. A clear understanding of working capital is a critical aspect of financial statement analysis. Pressures on working capital represent a valuable indicator of problems prior to slow debt service. For this reason, lenders need to evaluate working capital clearly using the financial statements.

This section will develop two perspectives of working capital, static and dynamic. The term working capital is used to mean both current assets (as in a short-term loan for working capital purposes) and net current assets (that is, current assets less current liabilities). Our concern will be to establish whether sufficient net working capital (subsequently to be called working capital) is available to support the sales level.

In a static sense (based on a balance sheet review), working capital is necessarily linked to the capital structure. As of a balance sheet date, the diagram in Figure 1 illustrates the relationship. Since the capital structure simply illus-

Figure 1—Balance Sheet Relationship of Working Capital to the Capital Structure

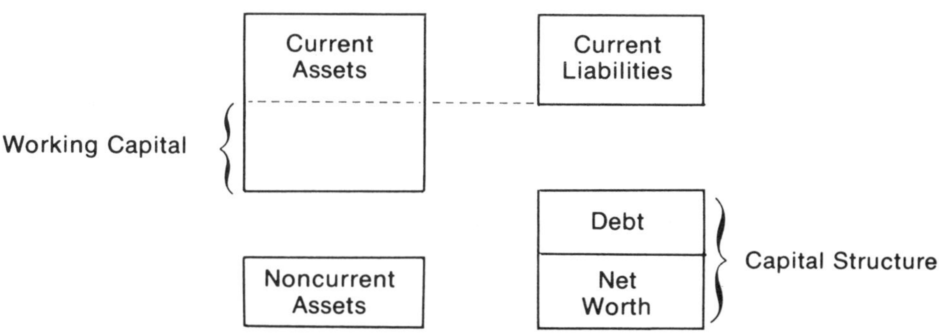

trates the source of capital committed beyond one year, *working* capital represents the portion of that capital that is constantly revolving through the business. The revolving issue will be further developed under the dynamic perspective.

The static view is used at the seasonal low point (when receivables and inventory are at minimum levels) to establish the ability of the capital structure to support the "permanent" or "core" assets of the firm. Short-term borrowed debt at that date is the key. If receivable and inventory turnovers represent minimum levels in relation to sales, the existence of any significant short-term debt (without corresponding "excess" cash) indicates pressure on working capital. The rationale is simply that if "core" assets must be liquidated to meet short-term debt in the short term, the inability to meet cash outflows *on schedule* (that is, cash inadequacy) is already apparent. Obviously, the time-tested proof of working capital adequacy is the ability to clear an unsecured line of credit for an extended period of time, preferably at the statement date, to ensure against simply shifting the burden to other creditors.

Several problems arise with the static perspective. One is secured debt made on a demand note. A lender who does not have confidence in the ability to service term debt out of cash generation over a reasonable term but who does have confidence in the secondary protection of current assets (particularly, receivables) may make a secured loan on a demand note. While the demand feature ensures the lender's ability to call the loan, it also means the debt will be classified as a current liability for statement purposes. Since part of such debt is revolving and supporting core needs, the working capital definition is distorted. Such debt is unlikely to be cleared. Another problem is the fact that the lender's view of this critical issue is limited to the number of balance sheets received during the year. This introduces the potential for "window dressing" through unusual receivable or inventory liquidations at statement dates. While historical turnovers are useful in establishing "normal" levels, a lender who represents the customer's only bank can employ the customer's borrowing record (that is, high borrowings, low borrowings, clearance periods) over the years. Average borrowings and deposits (possibly, overdrafts) may illustrate a growing reliance on bank debt to support working capital. The timing of high, low, and clean-up periods may help the lender to understand seasonal patterns.

The *dynamic* need for permanent working capital revolves around the typical lag between cash inflows and cash outflows. To illustrate a more dynamic perspective of working capital, the long-respected cash cycle analysis will be employed. The examples shown in Table 1 will assume that each firm has a sales rate of $1,000 per day and the turnovers are at the low point of a seasonal cycle (that is, core levels below which unusual circumstances would be required).

Table 1—Cash Cycle Illustrations

Captions	Companies A	B	C
1. Sales rate per day	$ 1M	$ 1M	$ 1M
2. Days sales in receivables	30	60	15
3. Days sales in inventory	60	90	0
4. Days in trading cycle (2 + 3)	90	150	15
5. Days sales in payables	−45	−30	−15
6. Days sales of working capital required	45	120	0
7. Receivable investment (1 × 2)	$30M	$ 60M	$15M
8. Inventory investment (1 × 3)	60M	90M	0
9. Trading cycle investment (1 × 4)	$90M	$150M	$15M
10. Payable support (1 × 5)	−45M	−30M	−15M
11. Required working capital support	$45M	$120M	0
12. Current ratio relationship (9 ÷ 10)	2×	5×	1×

It should be pointed out that the simplistic examples in Table 1 wash cash out with accruals and compute all turnovers with sales (as opposed to cost of sales for inventory) for consistency. However, the need for permanent working capital is caused by the necessary delay of cash inflows—as a result of uncollected sales (receivables) or necessary reinvestments in inventory—in satisfying current cash outflows that may be delayed somewhat. The three company examples illustrate that a required level of working capital will be solely dependent on these cycles. The cycles are influenced by the industry, setting up some external comparisons within the industry. But *no* absolute current ratio relationships exist.

The companies illustrated could have the following characteristics. Company A is an assembler of a fairly standard product. Many of the parts are purchased (giving rise to the high payables) and assembled (accounting for the reasonable inventory turnover). Thirty-day terms are given to customers. Therefore, at the rate of sales of $1,000 per day, Company A would require $45,000 of permanently available cash (that is, working capital) to avoid a cash shortage.

Company B produces a sophisticated, high technology product. Most costs are the skilled labor and engineering costs associated with specialized products. The extended production cycle is required by the individual work, and the low payable support is related to the relatively minor portion of sales dollars represented by purchased materials. All employees are paid weekly. Since the product must be set up at the customer's location and tested prior to becoming operational, extended receivable terms must be given. Although advance payments on specialized products are sometimes required in such cases, Company B would otherwise require $120,000 in working capital to support the significant lag between cash inflows and cash outflows.

Company C could be an advertising company or an insurance broker (most likely a service-oriented middleman). No inventory and spontaneous creditors willing to wait until cash is collected may eliminate the need for significant levels of working capital.

Such a dynamic approach is useful in distinguishing between a permanent and a short-term need. If Company A must build inventory to twice its low point prior to a selling season, such a temporary need would naturally be filled by short-term debt. However, if Company B's sales rate doubles to $2,000 per day, the doubling need for permanent working capital may easily lock a short-term bank loan into the company for an extended period.

In addition, the dynamic approach is a useful technique in understanding what the static current ratio relationship implies. If Company B had a current ratio of 2x, much of the need for working capital to cover, for a stable or growing company, the permanent void between inflows and outflows would have to be supported by short-term borrowed debt in an accounting sense. Such debt could only be cleared under the most undesirable circumstances (that is, unusual asset liquidation).

A successfully growing firm may, however, illustrate the capacity to service a term loan. Making a term loan (committing to the firm's capital structure for permanent working capital requirements) would satisfy the permanent need. While such pressures on working capital are otherwise the clearest sign of cash inadequacy, the borrowing power implied by an adequate collateral position may make the loan acceptable on a secured basis.

Evaluating working capital is complicated by the borrowing power issue. A firm that shows signs of working capital pressures but continues to have sufficient borrowing power to satisfy the problem has more of an academic than a real problem assuming interest can be covered. Otherwise, the working capital evaluation may be the best clue in the financial statements of a pending cash shortage. While it is certainly the most important analytical issue to any creditor getting paid in cash, it is also the most difficult to evaluate.

Short-term lending: What does short-term mean?

All appropriate financing is based on understanding the purpose of the loan. The purpose could be to buy seasonal inventory. Such a purpose usually implies a primary source of repayment (sale of the inventory in the ordinary course of the selling season) and a secondary source of repayment (forced liquidation of inventory at the best possible price). In addition, alternative protection may be available from other assets or owners. With legitimate short-term lending, it is usually presumed that the lender *can* get paid in the ordinary course of events in the short term (such as within a year). Thus, the lender requires a clear understanding of the working capital adequacy already discussed. If permanent working capital is inadequate, slow payment or continuous refinancing beyond a year should be anticipated. If cash generation is sufficient to service additional debt, a term loan may be more appropriate. If cash generation is unlikely to service the debt over a reasonable term without causing an identical problem, the loan may still be made on a strong collateral position. If working capital is judged to be adequate, flexible short-term lending is easily accomplished.

The elements of appropriate, short-term financing include:

1. Understanding the *specific* purpose.
2. Structuring the *maturity* in line with the *primary* source of repayment.
3. Identifying the *certainty* of secondary sources of repayment implicit in the purpose.
4. Evaluating alternative protection available from the balance sheet; and possibly
5. Ensuring access to secondary protection by taking security.

While the following discussion will be limited to general situations, the elements can be applied to any situation, no matter how specialized. As the alternative protection of a strong working capital position and clear borrowing power decline, the loan must be structured in line with the primary source of repayment so that slow payment initiates an inquiry by the lender. Secondary sources may continue to represent excellent protection, but collecting against secondary sources will force management to make decisions it might otherwise avoid. Showing interest may be all that is required.

Two types of facilities will be discussed, transaction loans and lines of credit. Normal recurring needs to support temporary (such as seasonal) receivables and inventories or to take cash discounts may justify a line of credit. The line may be disclosed or undisclosed (sometimes called a "guidance" line). Such purposes have primary sources of repayment that can easily be evaluated with the track record. To justify the flexibility of an unsecured line that could actually be used for anything, the firm must also illustrate an adequate working capital position. In addition, no significant changes in the firm's financial condition would be expected. If the leverage is high or subject to significant change, collateral may be required even if the line is otherwise considered short term.

Short-term transaction loans are typically made on time notes as the need arises. Such loans may actually be for "recurring" purposes, but because the lender has no clear track record to evaluate (for instance, in start-up or turnaround situations), a transaction loan would probably be appropriate. Otherwise, unusual needs (unusual buildup in receivables or inventory) or concentrated needs (loan to a contractor to support one receivable) should be satisfied with short-term notes structured in line with the expected end of the need. Thus, slow payment or refinancing should be accompanied by an explanation of what went wrong. Since the track record does not necessarily help evaluate such situations, the payment record more than financial statements must help monitor the credit. If the alternative protection in the firm is also weak, reasonable collateral may need to be taken to do the deal. Although demand notes may be used with collateral, using an unsecured demand note destroys the best monitoring technique available to a lender—the payment record.

Intermediate term lending: Does the purpose help pay the loan?

Intermediate term loans must be structured according to the productivity of the need and the availability of the primary source of repayment. The elements of appropriate intermediate financing are:

1. Understanding whether the specific *purpose* will be productive in *supplementing* cash generation.

2. Structuring the *maturity* in line with the availability of the primary source of repayment.

3. Identifying the certainty of secondary sources implicit in the purpose.

4. Evaluating alternative protection from existing cash generation (possibly diluted by additional interest), the financial condition, or guarantees.

5. Possibly, ensuring access to secondary protection by taking and controlling collateral when primary sources are uncertain, difficult to judge over the term, or subject to significant alternative demands (such as dividends).

While specialized types of financing such as leases and mortgage loans are part of this category, space limits the discussion to more common types of intermediate term financing. Term loans may be used for fixed-asset requirements (for example, equipment) that are expected to generate additional cash immediately. Term loans may also be used when the purpose may not be expected to supplement cash generation. If the purpose is to solve an existing working capital weakness, buy back stock, acquire the company, extend the maturity of existing debt, or support unproductive capital expenditures such as for pollution equipment, the cash generation indicated by the track record may not increase. Cash generation may actually decline as additional interest is introduced without expanding productive assets (for example, acquisitions, buying back stock, or unproductive investments). Thus, if the debt service becomes too much of a burden, the payment record will help the lender monitor the credit quality.

Term loans may be combined with revolvers or standbys under certain circumstances. Smaller buildings (that may not require the controls of construction financing) or equipment may not be productive in generating cash during a construction or start-up period. During that period, it is unreasonable to force repayment. Thus, the grace period, a standby credit, or possibly a revolver (for very good credits) may be used. Once cash generation starts, the lender ordinarily will put his claim on the cash flow by amortizing the loan. Permanent working capital requirements that result from successful growth may also justify a revolver and term loan. Such a facility does not require repayment during the revolving period acknowledging that much of the cash generation is tied up in growing receivable and inventory investments. Forcing repayment would reduce the growth potential. However, the capacity to pay under slower growth conditions must always be clear. The term loan puts the creditor's claim on the cash generation as it is expected to be available in the future.

Other important financing issues beyond the scope of this article are pricing, documentation, planning maturities, and specialized financing. Of course, pricing and documentation are secondary issues until the credit is judged to be acceptable and the loan is properly structured.

Borrowing power: A look at the balance sheet

Measuring borrowing power is a matter of identifying how much *additional* debt the firm may be able to attract and handle. If a firm can attract little or no additional debt, an unexpected setback could have serious consequences. To attract additional debt, a firm must be capable of servicing the debt. Debt to solve problems probably implies that no additional earning power would result. Thus, existing earnings would have to be able to cover higher levels of interest (perhaps, after adjusting discretionary expenses). The level of interest coverage is an obvious consideration. Beyond handling interest, sufficient excess cash generation over minimum demands must be available to service principal. While cash flow coverage of current maturities is often employed, the minimum demands of capital expenditures, working capital (under growth conditions), and possibly dividends on cash generation must also be considered. Although leverage relationships are often employed in evaluating borrowing power, debt must be serviced so no static leverage relationships necessarily apply.

General approach to financial analysis

Financial analysis represents the focal point of evaluating risk. Of course, understanding accounting represents a necessary evil. This section will briefly outline a general approach.

Evaluating operating successes and failures

Analysis ordinarily begins with sales which represent the principal cash inflow. The stability of trends and the rate of growth have implications for borrowing needs as well as the capacity to pay. Success is, however, measured by discretionary profitability, not sales levels. Discretionary profits, possibly including obvious adjustments such as profit sharing, must be able to cover volatile interest and provide sufficient cash generation to cover long-term needs. Economic and human considerations are obviously critical to understanding and anticipating gross and operating margins.

Interpreting financial consequences and decisions

Analysis generally moves from the income statement into the funds flow. The funds flow is the most underrated aspect of analysis. As defined, financial risk represents the inability of cash generation to meet the five demands previously discussed. The consideration begins with the trend in cash generation which is largely a summary of operating results. After adjusting for nonrecurring events, confidence in future cash generation is usually based on a stable rather than volatile trend.

Whether the level of cash generation is sufficient depends on the various demands. Some firms will need to meet significant demands for dividends, capital expenditures, debt service, and working capital. Others may have minimal demands for dividends, etc. Of course, the lender must attempt to distinguish between essential needs, such as required capital expenditures and contractual maturities, and reported expenditures which may be in part discretionary. Capital expansion and prepayments of debt would be examples of the latter. The funds flow analysis concludes with a change in working capital.

Using the best clue as to risk

A significant decline in working capital to cover long-term needs (established in the funds flow) or rapidly growing receivables and inventories (with sales) may easily lock short-term debt into the firm's capital structure. If cash generation is sufficient to justify refinancing, the pressure can be easily relieved. Or, if a strong collateral position exists, the loans may be secured. In either case, the pressures on working capital and on the ability to meet obligations on schedule are clear.

In addition to the inability to clear the line, the payment of trade debt may be delayed to the point that the actual need for working capital is vastly understated by short-term bank debt. Significant trade slowness is also a sign of working capital pressures and can only be established through trade services or investigation. Although working capital pressures are the best symptoms of cash inadequacy in financial statements, evaluating work capital in conjunction with borrowing power is an acquired skill. The previous discussion on working capital should help in developing it.

Projecting everything forward

Because lenders get paid in the future, financial statement analysis is only useful as an indicator of the future. If the track record is expected to represent a reasonable indicator of the future, this projection may be informal. If the size or circumstances of the loan or fundamental change in the human or economic elements reduces the value of the track record, formal projections may be required. Analyzing those projections follows a pattern similar to evaluating historical statements except such projections are statements of hope rather than fact. Projections should always be tested by considering lower sales, lower profit margins, higher interest, heavier inventory, and higher receivables which tend to be the most optimistic areas.

Estimating the options

Lenders always reach the point of considering the worst case. What if things do not work out as expected? This aspect can be called estimating the options. The static balance sheet strength is a part of this consideration. But although the leverage (debt to worth) may be low, the firm may not have the dynamic capacity to meet interest and principal. In such a case, additional debt may simply add to the problem. If some capacity to handle the debt is clear, a strong balance sheet or a balance sheet dominated by liquid and certain asset value such as the value of receivables may indicate the potential collateral available to ensure repayment. In addition, significant off-balance sheet value may justify borrowing power. Any reliance on off-balance sheet value must be accompanied by consideration of such off-balance sheet liabilities as guarantees and by some independent verification of such value (for example, an appraisal).

Making the credit judgment

Eventually, good lenders put the pieces of the puzzle together. They will arrive at a decision in their own way regardless of how similar their training may be. However, some difficulty often arises as the lender attempts to communicate that judgment to a senior lender, a loan committee, an examiner, etc. For this reason in part, risk ratings can be invaluable in positioning a credit on a risk spectrum.

Table 2 describes some characteristics that might be identified with various categories of risk. The issues down the left column follow roughly the topics previously discussed. Under each risk category ("high quality," "average," etc.), a general characteristic is described for each topic. These are designed principally to provoke thought, not to provide a checklist. Risk ratings are not intended to make arriving at a credit judgment any easier. On the contrary, they force a lender to think through a credit more precisely and completely. While many rating schemes use a narrow set of ratios to assist lenders, those ratios should never replace the conscientious consideration of all the facts before the lender. As a further point, a credit will rarely fit nicely into one risk category (column) for all issues. Thus, the lender must weigh the importance of each issue.

Deciding how to lend, monitor, and control

If a positive decision is made, the lender must always identify the sources of repayment implied by the purpose. The loan must also be put in the context of the firm. Thus, a short-term loan for seasonal inventory should be easily liquidated unless existing working capital pressures divert the funds realized to other needs. Although the firm's track record may appear sound, an aquisition or stock repurchase loan that replaces equity with debt will require existing profits to absorb more interest and existing cash generation to service more debt. An unusually large loan may fundamentally change the track record and require the success of the purpose of the loan. Such a situation would require the careful consideration of projections.

If some problem with payment is possible and perhaps likely, the maturity must be structured according to the primary source of repayment. In high risk situations, the limited access to cash implies that the subsequent problems will eventually affect the payment schedule. Thus, the lender is in a better situation to monitor problems on a current basis as opposed to awaiting financial statements that may arrive along after the problem occurs. Before the problem becomes so serious, the careful evaluation of financial statements, particularly the working capital, can indicate growing problems. (Knowing this, some borrowers may delay submission of financial statements which may present a clue to problems.)

Finally, the lender must exercise some control over the sources of repayment if any uncertainty exists. For term loans, loan agreement covenants may re-

Table 2—Risk Rating Characteristics for Bankable Credits

Issues	High Quality	Above Average	Average	Below Average	Increased Risk
Sales and earnings (historical and expectations if different)	• Stable/growing market • Stable sales growth and expectations • Significant earning power in relation to assets	• Market may be periodically subject to minor weakness • Sales follow or exceed market • Controlled growth and costs but periodic margin declines • Significant earning power in relation to assets on average	• Market may suffer periodic weakness or experience rapid growth • Sales follow market • Earning power may be average but subject to market weakness or contingent on growth	• Market may reflect more volatility or significant competition • Sales trend illustrates market or specific problems or risks • Earning power is low in relation to assets or volatile	• Market may be very mature, highly cyclical, or have intense competition • Sales trend may be very slow, subject to dramatic problems, or very rapid growth • Earning power in relation to assets is chronically low, declining, or subject to significant losses
Interest coverage (historical and expected component of borrowing power)	• Substantial interest coverage under all conditions or expected conditions	• Substantial interest coverage on average though may show minor weakness due to margin declines or rising rates	• More than adequate interest coverage on average but subject to periodic weakness	• Coverage is generally acceptable but subject to periodic pressures that may limit borrowing power	• Coverage is marginal, subject to periodic weakness, but managed, or limits significant added borrowing
Cash flow trends and demands (historical and expected debt servicing capacity)	• Strong and stable trend in cash generation • Significant internal financing of	• Cash generation may flatten or show minor declines but generally improves	• Cash generation illustrates slow growth, market pressures, or is contingent on	• Cash generation is very slow growing in relation to assets or volatile • High dividend	• Cash generation is low, declining, or significantly lagging asset growth

Table 2—continued

	asset growth • Cash flow ability to service term debt is strong and stable and able to support added term debt	• Capacity to service debt is consistently clear and significant on average • Dividends and asset control are reasonable	sales growth but is consumed by assets • Capacity to service debt is adequate on average	payouts • Capacity to service existing debt is acceptable on average but subject to pressures causing refinancing	• Excessive dividend payouts • Limited long-term debt and borrowing power due to inability to service over reasonable term
Working capital adequacy	• Consistent ability to clear bank lines • Efficient receivable and inventory turnovers • Payables on discount basis	• Consistently able to clear bank lines • Unusual receivable or inventory building associated with market may periodically increase proportionate usage	• Typically able to clear lines • Unusual building associated with market may prevent clearing periodically • Rapid growth may lock in short-term borrowings to be refinanced	• Periodic problems or diversion of cash may cause working capital pressures • Heavy reliance on short-term bank debt or payables is common	• Obvious working capital pressures • Reliance on adequately secured borrowings with periodic limits on borrowing power implicit in acceptable asset protection
Leverage (historical and expected margin for error in assets)	• Absolute level related to asset turnover • Reliance on borrowed debt is low in relation to ability to service • Leverage is stable and provides significiant asset (perhaps liquid) coverage of debt	• Leverage is generally stable but subject to temporary asset building that is subsequently controlled • Asset coverage is significant with perhaps a liquid asset base	• Leverage is slightly more volatile or marginally declining due to asset building or periodically weak earnings • Asset coverage is adequate on average and controlled after unusual building	• Leverage may be subject to uncontrolled asset growth periodically • Volatile earnings or high dividends may restrict equity growth • Asset coverage is dependent on less liquid assets but more than adequate collateral exists	• Leverage is high • Specific asset coverage of collateral for loans is acceptable • Repayment over reasonable term would be partially dependent on asset liquidation

strict alternative uses of cash generation through dividend restrictions (or owner guarantees), capital expenditure limits, and acquisition prohibitions. Covenants may protect the financial condition evaluated through financial ratios (worth to debt and current ratios), financial amounts (tangible net worth and working capital), and insurance coverage. Covenants may also protect the lender's position with regard to alternative creditors through negative pledge, negative debt, and cross-default clauses. If collateral is required, the status of collateral (particularly changing collateral such as receivables) should be reported regularly and checked for value by the lender. Periodically, the physical existence and quality of collateral should be verified by on-site visits or collateral audits.

A lender who properly structures, monitors, and controls loans going in will have much less trouble coming out.

Summary: No one said it was easy

Good commercial lending is an acquired skill. To acquire it, a lender must understand the technical areas of accounting, economics, and finance. However, only careful consideration (analysis) and deliberate decision-making (judgment) can lead to developing the necessary skill. All lenders make mistakes, but good lenders will learn from their mistakes. Such experience is invaluable to developing lending skill. Since, in the final analysis, most lenders are self-taught, the hope is that this article will help guide lenders through appropriate thought processes so that they can avoid learning the hard way. □

A Philosophical Foundation for Credit Analysis

by David B. Still

Although this article is geared for students of credit, commercial lenders at every level can benefit from its "back to basics" point of view. The author's purpose is to provide a philosophy of credit analysis—to present a simple definition of credit based on logical reasoning, rather than empirical methods. To that end, David Still focuses on three basic credit concepts: the viability of loan purpose, a first way out of the loan, and second ways out.

The author is senior vice president, The Philadelphia National Bank, Philadelphia, Pennsylvania.

Students of credit frequently seem to find themselves working aimlessly through myriad credit concepts and analytical techniques. With computer aids and modern mathematical tools, it is possible within minutes to conduct an extensive analysis of ratios, trends, margins, industry comparisons, working capital, liquidity, leverage, capital adequacy, asset turnover, and cash flow. The tools and aids of credit analyses have advanced to a sophisticated level; yet an improvement in the quality of analytical tools does not ensure an improvement in credit decision making. Many a credit student, after describing and reviewing pages of analytical data, has asked the same question: "How much capital and liquidity are enough, and how much are not enough?"

Without a basic philosophical understanding of what credit analysis is designed to accomplish, few students of credit can use the sophisticated tools and techniques in a meaningful manner. The fact remains that credit analysis is an art, not a science, and it is based on certain sound principles.

Is there a basic approach to credit analysis which is applicable to General Motors *and* Harry Jones' Grocery Store? The answer may lie with the three

---

The author dedicates this article to Frank R. Dyer, Jr., former chief lending officer at PNB and a past RMA president.

important concepts of viability of loan purpose, first way out, and second way(s) out. Once one truly understands the logic behind these three concepts, one can apply them to any loan situation.

Viability of loan purpose

Viability of loan purpose is the first principle of credit. Simply put, one must truly understand the events which give rise to the need to borrow. And under the test of "common sense," that purpose must make sense. An inadequate understanding of loan purpose due to a lack of data or to an intuitively nonsensical purpose are grounds for declining the credit request. To test this criteria, one should be able to explain the purpose of a credit to an uninformed nonbanker and have that purpose appear logical and sensible.

Common-sense test

While this concept may sound almost absurdly simple, many a credit analyst has failed this basic first test. How many times has one been faced with the answer "working capital" in response to "What is the purpose of this loan?" When applied to the common-sense test, working capital falls short. Clearly, working capital makes no intuitive common sense to anyone, much less an uninformed nonbanker.

An appropriate answer to the same question might go as follows: "XYZ Company manufactures Christmas tree balls all year but can only collect on its accounts receivable after the Christmas season. As a result, XYZ's accounts receivable and inventory expand until December, at which time they are converted into cash. During the expansion phase, XYZ needs to borrow and during the contraction phase the loans are repaid." This clearly stated loan purpose takes on a dynamic quality which allows one to relate to common sense.

Aside from being descriptively clear, the loan purpose should make sense in the context of the borrower's business, management, industry, and surrounding environment. For instance, it would be nonsensical to finance a new plant to manufacture obsolete buggy whips or to expand a chemical plant when information indicates that there is already 150% overcapacity in its product line.

At this point, many lenders might point out that many of their loan commitments are essentially insurance policies to be used only when commercial paper is unavailable, the borrower realizes operating losses, or it wishes to make an acquisition. Do these loan purposes make sense? They make sense only if the lender establishes clear guidelines for usage and is able to assess first and second ways out of the loan within those guidelines.

A clear understanding

It must be clear that specific, well-understood events give rise to the need to borrow. Dollars are fungible in a company, making it unrealistic to say that a dollar of loan was used to support a dollar of inventory. Instead, one must clearly understand what events gave rise to the need for the company to borrow. In summary, the purpose of every loan must be clearly understood, be economically viable, and make imminent sense.

First way out

The first way out of a loan should be tied to a reasonably predictable positive cash flow. Positive cash flows are generally associated with seasonality or profitability. Seasonality creates a short-term positive cash flow through the intrayear expansion and contraction of the trading assets as a company leaves then approaches its natural year-end. Profitability creates the opportunity for short-term and long-term positive cash flow. Examination of the specific aspects of seasonality or profitability in a loan situation is crucial to predicting a first way out.

Seasonality

Seasonality can be clearly described by a company's management. Any natural or artificial event which gives rise to uneven accumulations and contractions of trading assets (accounts receivable and inventory) can be described as seasonality. The term is commonly associated with harvests, unique buying terms, inventory availability, purchasing policy, market demand, datings, competitive selling terms, and many other factors. A common element from one company to the next is that the events which give rise to seasonality can be numerically measured by the size of the trading assets on the monthly balance sheets.

Seasonality is described, measured, and tested. A seasonal loan commitment should be out of debt during a company's natural year-end. If no clean-up occurs, one must view the first way out opportunities from a long-term cash flow standpoint. Last, a company that has no seasonality theoretically has no need for short-term loan commitments, except possibly for insurance purposes. Companies frequently set up lines to ensure against unexpectedly burdensome (from a cash flow standpoint) purchases of inventory, buildup in receivables, operating losses, or pension or tax payments. Steady short-term loans are essentially long-term loans in disguise. This brings us to the second conventional positive cash flow—profits.

Profits

Any nonseasonal loan's first way out should come from the positive cash flow associated with profits. Evidence of the predictability of profits comes from a rigorous review of past earnings performance and an extrapolation of that profile into the future. This review covers conventional credit concepts such as character of management, environmental and economic conditions, economics of the business, as well as a fundamental analytical review of the historic financial statements. Such analysis should be supported by company-supplied income projections and pro forma balance sheets with detailed assumptions regarding the business plan.

These forecasts merely quantify that which is being stated by the company: that there will be future positive cash flows sufficient to repay a loan. Analytically, there should be a margin in future years between net income estimates and obligatory debt service. The comfort margin is strictly a function of the degree of confidence that one has in the loan purpose and the supporting first-way-out analysis.

In summary, the first way out of a loan should be tied to the positive cash flow from short-term seasonality or long-term profits. When a loan is made, it is important to be honest as to the short- or long-term nature of its cash flow payback because the analytical review process is markedly different.

Second ways out

The second way(s) out of a loan should be tied to sound asset values. Whether a loan is secured or unsecured, asset protection is the third important principle in this credit philosophy. The key concept in determining asset value is that an asset's value is a function of its earning power. A sound credit analyst disregards the concepts of intrinsic and accounting value.

Asset value

In beginning an evaluation of the second way(s) out, one asks: "What will I do if there is no first way out, that is, the seasonality or profitability that was predicted fails to occur?" Every loan can and should have a worst-case strategy before a final decision to commit. There are myriad conventional second ways out of a loan. Among these ways are accounts receivable, equipment, real estate, inventory, and the stock of viable subsidiaries. The confidence that one has in the first way out and overall risk profile of the company dictates the degree to which second-way-out avenues are perfected in advance.

For example, highly leveraged, steady borrowers with little seasonality borrow against accounts receivable. These accounts receivable are thoroughly audited in advance to define a liquidation value or a sound second way out. Risky capital expansion loans are sometimes secured by equipment which has been appraised by an auctioneer for an "under the hammer" resale value. Real estate loans are conventionally supported by specialized appraisals of real estate to assess collateral value.

Last, many companies present asset value opportunities through their ability to sell off sound businesses. Every asset on the balance sheet can be analyzed for its ability to be converted into cash during adverse conditions, albeit such an assessment may reveal surprisingly low values when viewed from this perspective.

Legal aspects

Once asset value estimates are established as a second way out, the credit analysis task is not complete. Not only must the values exist but the lender must be able to gain control of the situation to realize those values for loan repayment. While the practical aspects of asset sales are assimilated in the value assessment, one must now review the legal aspects of the second way out.

There are many legal barriers to perfecting a second way out of a loan. Some of these legal considerations commonly faced are a company's legal structure and its effect on upstream and downstream guarantees; other lending agreements and indentures and their control over matters relating to pledging of assets, sale of assets, guarantees, dividends, management, etc.; laws covering the perfection of security interests; and the case history which has emanated from the bankruptcy courts. The final assessment of asset values as a second way out must be accompanied by quality legal counsel regarding the bank's ability to realize those values when they are needed.

Soundly conceived loans have a reasonably predictable second way out in case the first way out fails to materialize. The second way out should be tied to realizable asset values and exist in a legal environment which facilitates the execution of a predetermined collection strategy.

Conclusion

The foundation of a sound philosophical approach to credit analysis lies with the three credit concepts of viability of loan purpose, first way out, and second way(s) out. The fundamental analysis of ratios, trends, margins, industry comparisons, working capital, liquidity, leverage, capital adequacy, asset turnover, and cash flow is designed to improve one's understanding of one or all of these three principles.

Every loan should make common sense and have at least two ways of repayment. Loans that do not meet these criteria stand a good chance of resulting in a steady loan situation which will ultimately have to be worked out or written off. Every soundly conceived loan should have a viable loan purpose, show a positive cash flow as the first way out, and have asset protection as the second way(s) out. □

Author's update

In recent years, the concept of "lender liability" has added a new and potentially damaging factor into the lending process. Founded on legal theories such as fraud and duress, fiduciary duty, contract, good faith and fair dealing, and indemnity, lender liability subjects lenders to legal action, and potentially to damage awards, for the manner in which the lender conducts the lending arrangement with a borrower. All lenders should consult legal counsel on this concept, particularly in the context of analyzing a loan's second way out.

Working Capital and Cash Flow Analysis

Working Capital Theory Revisited

by Jeffrey W. Miller

In the following article, Jeffrey Miller takes issue with what has been the traditional formula for deriving working capital. He describes—and prefers—a different formula which states working capital in terms other than the difference between current assets and current liabilities. He goes on to discuss the sources and competing uses of working capital adequacy. And, finally, he takes some shots at the current ratio and suggests some alternatives to it.

At the time this article was first published in May 1979, the author was assistant vice president, Chemical Bank, Centereach, New York.

Working capital is probably the most frequently used term in lending, yet it escapes universal definition. To my customers, it is often the balance in their checking account or the funds used to operate their businesses or something else equally nebulous.

Unfortunately, bankers can be just as vague when queried about working capital. Each tends to have his own favorite definition. "Working capital is the difference between current assets and current liabilities," a banker will say. Or "it's the excess of liquid assets over current obligations."

The basic formula for deriving working capital—current assets − current liabilities = working capital—does not properly express what working capital is. More elaborate definitions, occasionally accompanied by eloquent discourses on accounting practices, also frequently misconstrue working capital theory.

This article placed first in a local paper writing competition sponsored by the New York Chapter of Robert Morris Associates in 1978.

Working capital theory, however, is the foundation of liquidity analysis, and an analysis of a company's liquidity circumstances is usually an important phase in making a credit decision. Proficiency in analyzing liquidity circumstances demands a sound understanding of working capital theory. Understanding what working capital is, where it comes from, what it is used for, and most important, how much a given company should have, are key aspects of working capital theory.

The purpose of this article is to clarify working capital theory, to suggest applications for analytical purposes, and to suggest some new ratio techniques for liquidity analysis. I will begin by defining working capital and will then consider its sources and competing uses. After that I will discuss how to determine working capital adequacy and will close with some thoughts on ratios that can be used in lieu of the current ratio.

Definition of working capital

Before we can agree on a definition of working capital, let's consider the common misconception that working capital is what you get when you subtract current liabilities from current assets. Obviously, that is a way to calculate precisely a dollar figure equal to a given company's working capital. In my opinion, however, that is almost like saying apples minus oranges equals pears since subtracting liabilities from assets is only a theoretical exercise. It cannot produce anything tangible other than perhaps net assets. I'd like to suggest that it would probably be better to define working capital in its own terms, rather than in terms of the difference between current assets and current liabilities.

Analogies with net worth

Before beginning such an approach to defining working capital, I would like to digress briefly and investigate some analogies with net worth. Net worth can be calculated by subtracting total liabilities from total assets. But to say that net worth is the *difference* between assets and liabilities is merely a restatement of the basic balance sheet equation.

I think a more appropriate definition of net worth would be something like "the owner's equity in assets," or "the investment of owners and earnings that has been retained in a business." Although such definitions are not refined, they are not uncommon explanations of net worth. And, beyond that, they are basically correct. They express net worth in its own terms, rather than as the difference between something and something else. In essence, since it is easier to conceive of net worth when defined in its own terms, it should be easier to conceive of working capital when defined in its own terms, rather than as the difference between two other commodities.

Several analogies become apparent when we look at the balance sheet equation and the basic formula for calculating working capital. The two formulas are usually stated as follows:

$$TA = TL + NW$$

and

$$CA - CL = WC$$

where current assets = CA, total assets = TA, current liabilities = CL, total liabilities = TL, net worth = NW, and working capital = WC.

By aligning the equals, plus, and minus signs, the two formulas can be restated to take on very similar appearances. Look at two of the possibilities:

$$TA = TL + NW$$
$$CA = CL + WC$$

or

$$TA - TL = NW$$
$$CA - CL = WC$$

I feel that the formulas now look quite alike, with assets, liabilities, and signs in comparable locations. The only differences are the substitutions of C for T and WC for NW. Since I am generally averse to expressing net worth or working capital in terms of *differences,* I would prefer not to use the second set of formulas. However, the first set of formulas (which contain no minus signs) could be defined in language similar to the basic formula I first gave for calculating working capital but without creating any misconceptions. Such definitions for these formulas are as follows: *Total assets are supported by total liabilities and net worth. Current assets are supported by current liabilities and working capital.* While the latter of these restatements begins to express what working capital does (supports current assets), it still fails to clarify what working capital is.

Expansion of balance sheet equation

To move closer to a meaningful definition of working capital, it becomes necessary to expand the balance sheet equation. Total assets, composed of current assets (CA) and fixed and all other assets (FA), can be symbolized as follows:

$$TA = CA + FA$$

Total liabilities, composed of current liabilities (CL) and long-term debt (LTD), can be symbolized as follows:

$$TL = CL + LTD$$

The balance sheet equation can therefore be symbolized in an expanded form as follows:

$$CA + FA = CL + LTD + NW$$

By making a few adjustments to this balance sheet equation, subtracting CL and FA from both sides, we can derive another formula for calculating working capital as follows:

$$CA - CL = LTD + NW - FA$$

or

$$WC = LTD + NW - FA$$

If we refer to LTD + NW as *permanent capital,* we could verbalize the latter of the above formulas as "working capital equals permanent capital minus fixed (and other) assets." But that still expresses working capital in terms of differences, so let's take the formula one step further. We will add back FA to both sides, reverse both sides of the equation, and create the following formula:

$$LTD + NW = FA + WC$$

Stating working capital exclusively in its own terms

We could verbalize this formula as "a company's permanent capital is invested in fixed (and other) assets and working capital." In other words, since some of a company's permanent capital is invested in fixed and other assets, a company's working capital is the permanent capital invested in current assets. While that happens to be my favorite definition, it can be expanded to state that "*working capital is the investment of a company's owners and term lenders in the company's current assets.*" Such a definition comes quite close to stating working capital exclusively in terms of its own. To understand working capital theory, I think it is extremely important to accept that definition. I think we should disregard the old notion that working capital is the difference between current assets and current liabilities. Instead, we should think of working capital as the capital permanently invested in or working to support current assets.

Perhaps the current liabilities create the confusion, for some portion of a company's current assets are (usually) financed by current liabilities. The level of current liabilities, however, has no bearing whatsoever on the level of working capital. If, for example, we extend a short-term loan to a company to buy inventory, both current assets and current liabilities increase by the exact amount of the loan—working capital remains unchanged. A short-term loan used to pay current obligations would have no net impact on current assets, current liabilities, or working capital. In short, transactions that affect only current assets or current assets and current liabilities in equal measure never influence the level of a company's working capital. The *only* way that working capital can change is as a result of a transaction that affects current assets or current liabilities as well as one of the elements in the formula, that is, net worth, long-term debt, or fixed assets.

Validity of new formula demonstrated

Before considering where working capital comes from, let's agree on the validity of the new working capital formula (NW + LTD − FA) by actually calculating working capital using ABC Company's balance sheet below:

December 31, 1977
ABC Company ($ 000's Omitted)

Current assets	110
Fixed & other assets	90
Total assets	200
Current liabilities	50
Long-term debt	30
Total liabilities	80
Net worth	120
Total liabilities & net worth	200

Using the old formula:

$$\begin{array}{ccccc} CA & - & CL & = & WC \\ 110 & - & 50 & = & 60 \end{array}$$

Using the new formula:

$$\begin{array}{ccccccc} NW & + & LTD & - & FA & = & WC \\ 120 & + & 30 & - & 90 & = & 60 \end{array}$$

Both formulas obviously provide us with precisely the same dollar figure for WC. However, the new formula begins to give us some insight into where working capital comes from.

Sources and competing uses of working capital

I would like to use the new formula's three components to consider how working capital is created. At the same time, let's consider competing uses for the various sources of working capital.

Net worth

The primary source of working capital happens to be the net worth in the formula. Anything that increases net worth is a source of working capital. Conversely, anything that reduces net worth reduces working capital. For example, if ABC Company made a $10,000 profit and retained that profit to increase net worth, working capital would increase by $10,000 to $70,000 as follows:

NW	+	LTD	−	FA	=	WC
130	+	30	−	90	=	70

An additional $10,000 investment from the company's owners would have had the same positive impact on net worth and working capital. Losses or other transactions that reduce net worth—paying dividends, purchasing treasury stock, or other forms of withdrawals—reduce working capital by the exact amount of the transaction.

Long-term debt

A company can also create working capital by borrowing on a long-term basis and employing the proceeds of the loan as support for current assets. Working capital will increase by the amount of additional long-term debt, that is, the long-term loan less any portion classified as current. Assume that ABC Company borrows $40,000 for working capital purposes on a four-year amortizing term loan. Working capital would increase by $30,000 ($10,000 of the loan would have been classified as the current portion of long-term debt) from $60,000 to $90,000 as follows:

NW	+	LTD	−	FA	=	WC
120	+	60	−	90	=	90

Using the old formula for the sake of comparison, current assets (cash) would increase $40,000 (the amount of the loan), current liabilities would increase $10,000 (the current portion), and working capital would increase $30,000 as follows:

CA	−	CL	=	WC
150	−	60	=	90

In the absence of profitability (or cash flow) to service long-term debt, working capital decreases as payments are made on term obligations.

Fixed and other assets

Working capital is sometimes created by the sale of fixed assets and will increase by the exact amount of the reduction of fixed assets. As companies grow, however, it is more likely that the fixed assets in the formula will be a competing use of the various working capital sources. For example, let's assume that ABC Company purchases $25,000 of machinery. Working capital would decline by $25,000 to $35,000 as follows:

NW	+	LTD	−	FA	=	WC
120	+	30	−	115	=	35

Now let's use the new formula to summarize several transactions to analyze how working capital is affected. Let's assume that during 1978 ABC Company had the following transactions:

(1) $10,000 profits were made.
(2) $ 4,000 dividends were paid.
(3) $40,000 was borrowed on a four-year term, $10,000 classified current.
(4) $ 7,000 of long-term debt was paid.
(5) $ 6,000 of other assets were sold.
(6) $25,000 of machinery was purchased.

Using the formula to summarize sources and uses of working capital, the transactions could be summarized as follows:

	NW	+	LTD	−	FA	=	WC
	120	+	30	−	90	=	+60 (12/31/77)
	10 (1)	+	30 (3)	+	6 (5)	=	+46 (sources)
−	4 (2)	−	7 (4)	−	25 (6)	=	−36 (uses)
	126	+	53	−	109	=	+70 (12/31/78)

Such a method for reconciling changes of working capital can be employed to highlight specific sources and uses as above. Or it can be used to summarize the net changes of the three components of the formula. We could say, for example, that during 1978, ABC Company's working capital increased by $10,000 due to a $6,000 increase of net worth and a $23,000 net increase of long-term debt, less a 19,000 net increase of fixed and other assets.

In summary, working capital has three general sources: transactions that increase net worth, transactions that increase long-term debt, and transactions that reduce fixed and other assets. And conversely, aside from its primary use for supporting current assets, there are three general competing uses for the sources of working capital: transactions that reduce net worth, payments (reductions) of long-term debt, and increases of fixed and other assets. Remember that working capital never changes as a result of transactions that affect only current assets or current assets and current liabilities in equal measure.

Closer look at uses of working capital

At this point, since the definition and source of working capital should be clear, let's look a little more closely at its uses.

Supporting current assets

Let's forget that we are bankers for the moment and put ourselves in the position of a company's management. In that position, we would have a good idea of the seasonal and budget levels of inventory, accounts receivable, cash, and any other assets that comprise our company's current assets. We would be well aware of the turnover velocities of these assets as well as our company's operating performance and capital expenditure and financing plans. Considering current liabilities, we would know what levels of trade credit are available and what levels of accrued expenses to anticipate, as well as levels of any other current obligations. With this information at hand, we could calculate how much working capital will be required to support our company's current assets.

For example, if we know what our firm, XYZ Company, has for a low point level of current assets and current liabilities, we could calculate our working capital need as follows:

XYZ Company ($ 000's Omitted)

Cash		75
+ Accounts receivable		320
+ Inventory	400	
− Accounts payable	280	120
+ Other curent assets		35
− All other current liabilities		60
Required working capital		490

Our balance sheet would reflect current assets of $830,000 supported by $340,000 of current liabilities. Our current assets would also require $490,000 of working capital support. In essence, $490,000 would have to come from XYZ

Company's owners and term creditors to support an $830,000 level of current assets. Permanent capital of $490,000 would have to be invested in current assets.

In the preceding calculation, I have subtracted accounts payable from inventory, since accounts payable are usually considered a direct source of inventory financing. Any inventory not supported by trade credit requires working capital support. Accrued expenses, however, cannot be considered as direct financing of any specific current asset, hence they would be netted out last. In essence, we could say that a company uses working capital to support its current assets, less any direct trade credit support for inventory and less any indirect financing provided by accrued expenses and other current obligations.

Using working capital for bankers' analytical purposes

Now, as bankers, how can we use working capital theory for analytical purposes? I think the best application is determining the adequacy of a given company's working capital. It is fairly easy to identify trends in liquidity by comparing a company's statements over several accounting periods. Changes in working capital, current and quick (acid test) ratios, inventory turnover, accounts receivable collection period, and so forth can all be readily identified. But to say that a company's condition is very liquid, marginally liquid, marginally illiquid, or very illiquid can be a much more difficult task.

Our observations of trends can lead us to a subjective conclusion about liquidity. For example, if all the ratio and turnover trends are improving, we might conclude that a company's liquidity circumstances are strong. But if the company's condition had been illiquid to begin with, it might only be a little bit less illiquid at present. Conversely, if the trends are negative, we might conclude that liquidity is weak. Both conclusions could be wrong. A working capital adequacy approach, however, can lead us to a much more objective opinion of a company's liquidity circumstances. If we can determine how much working capital a given company should have, we can compare our calculation with the company's actual working capital level and make a credit judgment accordingly. I approach the question of working capital adequacy in much the same way as we did when playing the role of XYZ Company's management.

The cleanup philosophy

Before we make actual calculations, let me explain why we need to work with the low point level of current assets and current liabilities. Very basically, the low point level is used because of the "cleanup" philosophy. We generally expect that a company should be able to function in the absence of short-term bank borrowings (or at some designated minimum level of bank debt when several banks make available lines of credit) for some period. Traditionally, this period would be 30 days at a minimum, over any twelve months. The cleanup or low point of bank borrowings usually occurs when current assets are at their lowest levels. The actual low point usually occurs sometime between the seasonal inventory low point and the seasonal receivables low point. At that point, a company's base working capital can be derived exactly as we did in the XYZ Company example.

Making actual calculations and adjustments for various circumstances

The current asset levels can be calculated objectively by using antecedent financial statements, current information regarding collection experience and inventory turnover, and any other relevant information available. From antecedent financials, agency sources, trade checkings, industry surveys, and any other relevant sources, we can make determinations about the normally available levels of trade credit support and accrued expenses, as well as other current obligations. It is important to recognize discrepancies between available levels of current obligations and actual levels, since cleanup philosophy dictates that a company should remain current with all other creditors while in a cleanup cycle.

Once a base working capital figure has been derived, we may make several adjustments to account for the following possible circumstances:

(1) Profit and cash flow trends may dictate that a company needs additional base working capital to cover potential losses or shortfalls on debt service. Remember the competing uses. If net worth goes down, so does working capital. And, if cash flow is not adequate to service debt runoff, working capital would be depleted by the shortfall.

(2) Planned or necessary capital expenditures may not be fully funded by new term credit, requiring additional working capital equal to the difference between the cost of the new fixed asset and the term financing of it.

(3) The quality of a company's current assets may be questionable, which would necessitate additional base working capital to cover potential value declines. Accounts receivable charge-offs and loss provisions, as well as write-offs of unsalable merchandise, reduce net worth and working capital.

(4) Any known contingencies which are not mitigated by insurance, guarantees, bonding, etc. that could deplete a company's cash position will also re-

duce working capital. For example, if a company stands to lose a $50,000 lawsuit, it had better have $50,000 excess base working capital available, or it may have its liquidity strained.

(5) Long-term growth creates a need for additional working capital. Working capital must usually increase in direct proportion to sales growth, since higher inventory and receivables levels can be expected. If a company's cash flow, after debt service has been accounted for, does not provide working capital growth in proportion to sales increases, an excess working capital need is created.

(6) Highly seasonal companies may also require a higher base level of working capital to support a portion of their seasonal growth. The additional working capital depends on the company's historic conversion cycle success, the length of the cycle, and the degree of seasonal buildup.

Assessing a company's liquidity

Very seldom do companies have a working capital base adequate to accomplish all of the above objectives. Such a company would be in a very liquid condition and would be a minimal risk credit for seasonal financing. *It is the extent of the variance between a company's actual working capital, and what we calculate to be its necessary base working capital, that influences our conclusion about a company's liquidity.* For example, if we calculate that a company should have a $200,000 working capital base, and its actual working capital is $180,000, I would call that company relatively liquid. I would not be alarmed by a 10% deficiency. However, if its actual working capital was only $120,000, a 40% deficiency, I would be extremely reluctant to extend unsecured short-term credit. Such an illiquid situation might warrant collateralized loans, possibly liens on receivables and inventory, or a term financing to build working capital. But short-term unsecured credit would be difficult to justify.

A specific example

Let's consider a specific example, using XYZ Company, and calculate what level of base working capital it should have to be a low risk credit. Assume that all of the figures in the calculation are soundly based on a thorough understanding of the company's past and present financial circumstances. As such they will vary little from what XYZ's management calculated earlier. Assume further that XYZ Company has requested a $200,000 line of credit to support seasonal inventory and receivables buildups.

XYZ Company ($ 000's Omitted)

Minimum cash position		70
Low point accounts receivable		330
Low point inventory	400	
Less available trade credit	300	100
Other current assets		40
Net current assets		540
Less available accrued expenses		−80
Minimum base working capital required		460
Plus additional working capital requirements for:		
1. Profit/cash flow instability		0
2. Planned capital expenditures less direct financing		0
3. Quality concerns regarding current assets (assume slow receivables)		40
4. Known contingencies		0
5. Long-term growth requirements		0
6. Seasonal growth requirements		0
Required base working capital		500

By this calculation, XYZ Company should have a $460,000 working capital base to support its low point current asset structure. Since receivables slowness had been detected, possibly by an analysis of turnover ratios, aging schedules, and so on, the base figure was adjusted by $40,000. No other adjustments were deemed necessary. We can presume that cash flow from operations had been historically adequate to cover any required debt service, capital expenditures, and working capital growth requirements. Losses were not anticipated, and there were no known contingencies requiring additional base working capital.

No adjustment was made in the above calculation to account for seasonal growth. The degree of seasonal growth that would necessitate such an adjustment is very much a subjective judgment. It is a question of what proportion of a company's seasonal growth should be financed by substituting bank credit for working capital and seasonal trade credit buildup. A liberal lender may finance 100% of the seasonal needs because of his confidence in the company's ability to complete the conversion cycle. A conservative lender will be inclined to look for additional working capital to finance some portion of the seasonal growth. Having calculated a $500,000 base working capital need, I felt no adjustment was necessary for a $200,000 loan request. For a more substantial request, I might have made an adjustment. I will clarify the point at which an adjustment might be made when we discuss liquidity ratios in the pages ahead.

Determining if working capital is adequate

Once a working capital requirement has been calculated, compare that calculation with the company's working capital. For example, if XYZ Company had actual working capital of $450,000, $50,000 (or 10%) short of the $500,000 base requirement in our calculation, there would be some concern but no panic. The deficiency could be absorbed by a combination of tightening cash positions, cutting inventory slightly, and a marginal slowing of payments to trade and other current creditors.

Actually, a slight working capital deficiency can sometimes be viewed as shrewd employment of working capital or efficient cash management. That is, the company functions at a higher volume than its working capital can totally support without creating any severe strains. Modest working capital deficiencies will usually dictate upward adjustment of a loan's pricing rather than a declination or restructuring of the requested credit. Beyond a slight deficiency, however, I become concerned about a company's ability to accomplish a cleanup, while satisfying other creditors and without cutting inventory or other current assets below required levels.

XYZ Company, with a $450,000 base would appear to be reasonably liquid, and from a liquidity standpoint, a reasonable credit risk. However, if XYZ's working capital were substantially less than $450,000, I would consider obtaining a security interest in the company's assets. I might also prepare to accept a more permanent lending position, either receivables financing or term financing arrangements. The working capital base would not be adequate to warrant short-term unsecured credit.

The working capital adequacy approach can be a very enlightening method for making an overall evaluation of liquidity circumstances—much more enlightening than merely viewing ratio trends. As a lender, I would much rather conclude that a company has a solid working capital base, than determine that its current ratio has improved for three years in a row.

Basic deficiency of current ratio and some alternatives

I would like now to consider what I feel is a basic deficiency of the current ratio and some alternatives to it. However, first I would like to go back to our net worth analogies for a moment. From the standpoint of a creditor, net worth is frequently viewed as a cushion, the amount of value decline a company's assets can suffer or the amount of losses that can be absorbed before the assets are worth less than the outstanding liabilities. While net worth is a cushion to all creditors, working capital can be viewed as a cushion to current creditors. This analogy leans towards a liquidation viewpoint, that is, if the company fails, this is what we can expect.

From a going concern viewpoint, net worth is compared to the level of debts to create a proportion to evaluate risk in a somewhat different light. The leverage ratio (debt to equity ratio) indicates risk as the relative degree of debt versus equity support of a company's assets. Changes of the leverage ratio indicate changes of the relative degree of risk attached to financing the company.

The current ratio is too frequently viewed from a liquidation standpoint. A 2.0 ratio is often thought of as current assets twice covering current liabilities or as current assets that can shrink by 50% while current creditors can still be paid. Current assets are viewed as being available for paying current liabilities, when actually only cash (usually only a small percentage of current assets) can pay any liability. Also, as a proportion of assets to liabilities, the current ratio can create the same type of confusion that evolves from the CA − CL = WC formula. Using the current ratio is something like dividing apples by oranges.

One alternative to current ratio: working capital leverage ratio

Obviously the current ratio has its application, and through the years, it has been accepted as one of the best liquidity monitoring devices. Nevertheless, in setting up a proportion of current assets to current liabilities, I feel that many lenders are not totally comfortable with what the current ratio tells them. However, if we carry the net worth analogy to its logical conclusion, we can create a working capital leverage ratio to apply in place of the current ratio.

A ratio of current liabilities to working capital is analogous to the leverage ratio of total liabilities to net worth. While the leverage ratio expresses the riskiness of the overall capital structure (how total assets are supported—debt versus equity), a working capital leverage ratio would express the riskiness of the current capital structure (how current assets are supported—current liabilities versus working capital). Below are three examples of how the current ratio would compare with a working capital leverage ratio:

CA	–	CL	=	WC	$\frac{CA}{CL}$	$\frac{CL}{WC}$
(1) 300	–	100	=	200	3.00	.50
(2) 400	–	200	=	200	2.00	1.00
(3) 500	–	400	=	100	1.25	4.00

While a leverage ratio of .5 is generally thought to indicate relatively low overall risk, a .5 working capital leverage ratio would likewise indicate relatively low liquidity risk (versus a 3.00 current ratio). A 1.00 ratio would indicate that there is a 1 to 1 proportion of current liabilities support to working capital support of current assets. And a 4.0 ratio, as with the higher risk attached to a 4.0 leverage ratio, would indicate a fairly high liquidity risk.

Comparing a company's leverage ratio and working capital leverage ratio

By comparing a given company's leverage ratio with its working capital leverage ratio, we can to some degree identify what aspects of a company present the greater risks. For example, a company with a leverage ratio of 2.0 and a working capital leverage of 3.0 would have a riskier financing structure for its current assets than its overall asset structure. Conversely, a leverage ratio of 4.0 and a working capital leverage ratio of 1.5 would be indicative of overall high leverage but a somewhat less risky current situation.

Other alternatives to current ratio

Besides the working capital leverage ratio, at least two other alternatives to the current ratio exist, both of which would seem to be easier to understand than the current ratio. First, a ratio of current liabilities to current assets (the reciprocal of the current ratio) would indicate what percentage of current assets are supported by creditors. Saying that a company has 40% of its current assets financed by current creditors seems to make at least as much sense as saying the current ratio is 2.5. A second ratio, a ratio of working capital to current assets, would indicate what percentage of current assets are supported by working capital. As with the reciprocal of the current ratio, it would seem easier to accept that 60% of a company's current assets is supported by working capital than saying the company's current ratio is 2.5. While both of these ratios have merit, my preference would still be the working capital leverage ratio due to its analogy to the leverage ratio.

A working capital leverage ratio also serves analytical purposes quite well when setting up pro forma statements. As I mentioned earlier, when discussing the adequacy of XYZ Company's working capital base, the rationale for not adjusting the working capital base for seasonal requirements would be clarified. Using the working capital leverage ratio, we can set up pro forma statements to show the impact on XYZ's liquidity of a $200,000 loan and a matching $200,000 buildup of trade credit as follows:

XYZ Company ($000's Omitted)

	Low point	High point
CA	830 + 400	1,230
− CL	340 + 400	740
WC	490	490
WC Lev. Ratio	.69	1.51

In XYZ's case, the high point leveraging of working capital one and a half times was deemed satisfactory—the liquidity risk of a 1.51 working capital leverage was considered an acceptable risk. In essence, the ratio can be used to identify a cutoff point for financing seasonal inventory and receivables build-ups. In the same way that the leverage ratio is used to monitor the overall relationship of debt to equity (as a frequent term loan covenant, for example), the working capital leverage ratio can be used to monitor what levels of current debt are acceptable in relation to working capital.

If in my analysis of a company's overall financial circumstances I feel a company is an acceptable risk at 1.5, I am defining a credit limit. Suppose XYZ Company had been seeking a $300,000 line of credit in partial support of a $500,000 seasonal buildup with 1.51 having been established as the maximum permissible working capital leverage. I would have sought an additional $40,000* working capital investment versus a $260,000 facility based again on the XYZ Company example at the top of page 31.

* Actually, a $39,880.48 additional working capital requirement would have been identified by our formula

$$NWC = \frac{CL + F - R\,(WC)}{1 + R}$$

where NWC is new working capital, CL is low point current liabilities, F is the overall financing requirement, R is the maximum working capital leverage ratio, and WC is beginning working capital as follows:

$$NWC = \frac{\$340{,}000 + \$500{,}000 - [1.51\,(\$490{,}000)]}{1 + 1.51}$$

$$NWC = \frac{\$840{,}000 - \$739{,}900}{2.51}$$

$$NWC = \frac{\$100{,}100}{2.51}$$

$$NWC = \$39{,}880.48$$

	XYZ Company ($000's Omitted)	
	Low point	**High point**
CA	830 + 500	1,330
− CL	340 + 460	800
WC	490 + 40	530
WC Lev. Ratio	.69	1.51

In the absence of the additional working capital investment, $300,000 facility might still have been approved—but only at a higher interest rate to account for the higher risk. A more appropriate structuring for a $300,000 borrowing requirement might have been to establish a $200,000 credit line and provide the $100,000 balance with a working capital term loan.

Summary

In closing, let me simply summarize some of the highlights of working capital theory and my opinions regarding its application for analytical purposes:

(1) Working capital is the investment of a company's owners and term lenders in the company's current assets.

(2) The WC = NW + LTD − FA formula for calculating working capital gives us more insight into the sources of working capital than does the WC = CA − CL formula.

(3) There are three basic sources of working capital and, aside from supporting current assets, there are three competing uses.

(4) Transactions that affect only current assets or current assets and current liabilities in equal measure never affect working capital.

(5) Determining the adequacy of a given company's working capital base is a sound technique for assessing a company's liquidity.

(6) A cleanup should occur without riding the trade and other current creditors.

(7) A working capital leverage ratio may be more easily understood than the current ratio due to its analogy to the leverage ratio, and consequently, it will have more applications. □

Cash Flow—The Most Critical Issue of the 1980s

by James E. Perry, Ph.D.

James Perry feels that analyzing a firm's cash flow or liquidity is a critical issue that must be addressed in the credit analysis of a firm. And cash flow, according to Perry, is best reflected in the statement of liquidity, financing, and investment activities which he describes in the following article.

The author is associate professor of finance, University of Oklahoma, Norman. At the time this article was first published in September 1982, he was dean of the School of Business, Central State University, Edmond, Oklahoma.

In the decade of the 1980s, one of the most critical issues for business managers, if not *the* most critical issue, is that of liquidity. In the decade of the 60s, the accent was on profitability and justifiably so. From the late 50s throughout the 60s, inflation ranged from less than 1% to slightly more than 5% per year. During the same period of time, the prime rate ranged from a low of 2¼% to a high of 8½%. In short, because of the stability of the economic environment, management accented profitability and treated the issue of liquidity with benign neglect. Why not? The period of the 1960s was of great prosperity for our country. Even those managers who were not quite as adept at turning a profit as their competitors were able to stay in business and do quite well by simply riding the coattails of the bullish economy.

In the mid 1970s, the economic environment changed markedly. Whereas the average rate of inflation for the decade of the 60s was 2.3%, as measured by the

---

This article is based on remarks made by the author at a meeting of RMA's North Central Chapter in February 1982.

Consumer Price Index, inflation in the 1970s ranged from 3.3% to 11¼%. The prime interest rate during this same period rose to 11¾%. In short, the word "uncertainty" instead of the term "bull market" became the descriptive term for the economy. The significance from a management point of view was that no longer could management afford the luxury of accenting profitability while treating liquidity as a passive variable. The bottom line now meant managing revenues and expenses to achieve the desired level of profit while at the same time managing the cash inflows and outflows of the firm so as to maintain an appropriate level of liquidity.

Importance of liquidity

Broadly defined, liquidity deals with the cash inflows and cash outflows patterns of the firm. From a lender's point of view, a narrower definition of liquidity is the ability of the firm to service and repay its borrowed funds. Figures 1 and 2, which give the financial data for Longhorn, Inc., illustrate the importance of the issue of liquidity.

Sample financial statements

When presented with a loan request, every lender has his or her own technique for evaluating the request. If Longhorn, Inc. were to request a $150,000 loan with a three-year payout, at prime and unsecured, one might very well begin analyzing the request by double checking the profitability of the firm and then perhaps double checking its net working capital. In the case of Longhorn, a quick perusal of the income statement shown in Figure 1, indicates the firm is profitable with profits in 1979 of $43,000 and in 1980 of $54,000.

In the case of net working capital, there is clearly an excess of current assets over current liabilities. In 1979, net working capital is $105,000 while in 1980 it is $77,000 (see Figure 2).

Having double checked the profitability and net working capital position of the firm, a traditional calculation for the banker is to determine the sum of net income plus depreciation and label this sum perhaps as cash flow.

Funds-based versus cash-based calculations

Interestingly enough, the banker lends cash and wants cash back in repayment. Equally interesting, profitability and net working capital as well as the calculation of net income plus depreciation are not *cash-based.*

Net working capital is a *funds-based* concept. It is simply a quantity—an excess of current assets over current liabilities. It reflects only a quantitative difference and says nothing whatsoever with respect to the quality of the cur-

Figure 1—Income Statements—Longhorn, Inc.
(Amounts in Thousands)

	Fiscal Year Ending December 31 1979	1980
Net Sales	$2,267	$2,886
Cost of Goods Sold	1,881	2,366
Gross Profit on Sales	386	520
Operating Expenses:		
Executive Salaries	41	59
Depreciation*	8	12
Other Operating Expenses	250	338
Total Operating Expense	299	409
Net Income From Operations	87	111
Interest Expense	17	20
Net Income Before Taxes	70	91
Taxes	27	37
Net Income After Taxes	43	54

	Reconciliation of Retained Earnings 1979	1980
Beginning Retained Earnings	$ 35	$ 40
Net Income	43	54
Less: Dividends	(38)	(54)
Ending Retained Earnings	$ 40	$ 40

* Depreciation will be increased to $12,000 during 1980 to allocate the previous cost of the new building over future years and to include previously owned furniture and equipment in the new amount of annual depreciation.

---

rent assets of the firm. True, since the concept of net working capital deals with current assets and current assets are certainly expected to be converted into cash, one could suggest that there is a relationship between the level of net working capital and the ability of the firm to meet its short-term obligations. However, such a suggestion might be very imprecise at best in that the issue of being able to meet one's obligations is a function of the timing of the conversions that are expected to take place within the current asset category as well as the quantities that are converted. Only when the timing of the conversions is carefully assessed can any appropriate inferences with respect to the ability of the firm to meet its obligations be drawn.

Profitability obviously deals with the relationship between revenues and expenses. However, in that revenues include credit sales and expenses include

Figure 2—Balance Sheets—Longhorn, Inc.
(Amounts in Thousands)

	December 31 1979	1980
Assets		
Cash	$ 42	$ 34
Accounts Receivable	617	886
Reserve for Bad Debts	(48)	(122)
Inventory	104	194
Total Current Assets	715	992
Building and Equipment	56	96
Accumulated Depreciation	(36)	(48)
Net Fixed Assets	20	48
Total Assets	$735	$1,040
Liabilities and Net Worth		
Notes Payable—Banks	$100	$ 200
Mortgage Note Payable	0	35
Accounts Payable	500	662
Accruals	10	18
Total Liabilities	610	915
Common Stock	85	85
Retained Earnings	40	40
Total Net Worth	125	125
Total Liabilities and Net Worth	$735	$1,040

payables, the concept of profitability is also funds-based. So too, the sum of net income plus depreciation is a funds-based calculation.

Is the fact that net income plus depreciation is a funds-based concept important? Yes! Consider the journal entries that are shown in Figure 3. As simple as they may be, they could very well have been the source from which the 1980 income statement was derived. The fact is they fit. The fact is also that the word cash is not even used in any of the journal entries! Consequently, the suggestion that net income plus depreciation is in fact cash flow is speculative at best. Net income plus depreciation is a funds-based concept, not a cash-based concept. The difference is one of distinction. By way of analogy, we can say that just as all women are people, but not all people are women that all cash is funds, but not all funds are cash!

Figure 3—Journal Entries: Income Statement 1980

Journal Entry	Debit	Credit
Accounts Receivable	$2,886	
Sales		$2,886
Purchases	$2,425	
Executive Salaries	59	
Operating Expenses	338	
Interest Expense	20	
Accounts Payable		$2,425
Salary Payable		59
Operating Expense Payable		338
Interest Payable		20
Tax	$ 37	
Tax Payable		$ 37
Depreciation	$ 12	
Accumulated Depreciation		$ 12

Why have we used net income plus depreciation? If the calculation is not precise, that is, if it does not reflect cash flow, why have we used it and why have we stood by it so long?

The explanation is really quite simple. Net income plus depreciation has been used as a surrogate for cash flow because of the tax shield/tax exposure concept. As shown in Figure 4, revenues and certain expenses are tax-exposed; that is, the net impact on the firm is the amount of the revenue or expense times one minus the corporate tax rate. Other expenses, such as depreciation, which is not cash-related, have an impact on the firm equal to the amount of the deduction times the corporate tax rate. The sum of the net of the tax-exposed items and tax shield items equals the totals of net income plus depreciation. Theoretically, therefore, if the firm collected its revenues and paid its expenses without any time delays, the sum of the tax exposure and tax shield items would equal the net income plus depreciation, and the total would, indeed, reflect the cash flow of the firm.

Have you ever heard of a company that collected all of its revenues or paid all of its expenses without any time delays? In essence, have you ever heard of an all-cash business? Sometimes people suggest a liquor store or a fast food outlet would be such a business. True, these businesses continually take cash in, but do they have any salary payable, any rent payable, any interest payable?

Some people, of course, say that it really doesn't matter. In the end, it will all wash out. In other words, in the end, no matter what you say, net income plus depreciation will equal the cash flow of the firm. These people are, in fact,

Figure 4—Example: Tax Shield/ Tax Exposure Concept

Net Sales	\$2,886 (1 - t)* 2,886 (1 - .406)	\$1,714
Total Expenses (Cash-Related)	\$(2,783) (1 - t) (2,783) (1 - .406)	\$(1,653)
Depreciation	\$12 (t) 12 (.406)	\$ 5
	Total	\$ 66
	Net Income	\$ 54
	Depreciation	\$ 12
	Total	\$ 66

* t = corporate tax rate of 40.6%.

correct! However, where is the end? If the period of time we are talking about goes from the day God created the earth to the day of the big fire, on the final day, the net income plus depreciation will indeed equal cash flow. If, however, we are dealing with an intervening period such as 1982, or such as the second quarter of the fiscal year or the month of May, etc., we have problems. Are the problems significant? Only if you attach a due date to your promissory note! If the loan agreement specifies that the borrower may pay whatever he or she can at whatever points in time he or she can, the distinction between the cash flow of the firm and the calculation of net income plus depreciation is probably unimportant. However, has there ever been such a flexible loan agreement?

One last note. One could suggest that net income plus depreciation is cash flow as long as the business had no changes in any balance sheet items from one period to the next. Again, the suggestion is correct. However, have you ever witnessed a situation where a firm had no changes from one period to the next?

Calculating cash flow

How can you calculate the cash flow of the firm? First, we have to consider a very important fact. When an accountant prepares financial statements, the accountant is privy to the books of original entry of the firm. That is, the accountant is fully aware of all of the information that has fallen within the spectrum of operations of the firm. A financial analyst, however, deals with financial information after the fact. That is, a financial analyst begins the task of analysis when the financial statements are, in fact, submitted. The financial analyst, therefore, is not privy to the journals of the firm. Consequently, a financial analyst can only determine the cash flow of the firm by examining the balance sheets and income statements submitted, by integrating them so as to relate each income statement account with its related balance sheet account(s).

Statement of changes in financial position

Is there a financial statement specifically intended to aid in the identification of the cash flow of the firm? Yes! The statement of changes in financial position is specifically intended to serve this purpose. This statement, by the way, has traditionally been called the funds flow statement. For that matter, in the old days, accountants referred to it as the "where got, where gone" statement.

In essence, the statement of changes in financial position has three specific purposes. First, the statement is supposed to comment on flows from operations not otherwise discernible from traditional financial statements. The implication of this statement is that there are some flows which are not shown on any traditional statement such as the income statement. In other words, perhaps the income statement shows funds flows whereas the other flows that are implied could take the form of cash flows. Second, the statement of changes in financial position is supposed to comment on the financing activity of the firm. Financing decisions are very special. They are actively discussed, debated, and decided on at the very highest management levels within the firm. Third, the statement of changes in financial position is supposed to comment on the investment activity of the firm. Like financing decisions, investment decisions are discussed, debated, and decided on at the very highest levels of management within the organization. These kinds of decisions are typically unlike labor/personnel decisions which may be reversible. Financing and investment decisions are quite often irreversible, involve significant dollar values and have an impact on the firm which extends well into the future.

The statement of changes in financial position can be developed in terms of the change in net working capital from one point in time to another. This format, in fact, has been the traditional format that has been offered by the accounting community. To the extent, of course, that the economy was stable and that management was able to accent profitability and treat the issue of liquidity with benign neglect, a statement of changes in financial position constructed in the terms of the change in net working capital was acceptable to all parties. The fact remains, however, that such a statement again reflects only a change in quantity of net working capital and does not speak at all to the issue of cash flow. In fact, the only consideration with respect to cash flow is the idea that the statement shows the balances in the current accounts which obviously are expected to be converted in the short term.

Again, bankers lend cash and want cash in repayment. They don't lend funds and they don't lend net working capital.

Statement of liquidity, financing, and investment activities

An alternative format for the statement of changes in financial position is shown in Figure 5. This format is called the statement of liquidity, financing, and investment activities. In essence, the statement incorporates the three purposes of the statement of changes in financial position with its title. The statement begins with the balance in the cash account at the beginning of the

Figure 5—Statement of Liquidity, Financing, and Investment Activities for Longhorn, Inc. For the Period Ended 12/31/80

	Operations	Management Discretion	Total
Beginning Cash Balance			$ 42
1 Collections from Operations	$2,691		2,691
2 Other Resources Provided			
Notes Payable Bank		$100	100
Mortgage Payable		35	35
Total Resources Provided	$2,691	$135	$2,868
1 Payments for Operation			
Purchases	$2,294		$2,294
Salaries	59		59
Operating Expenses	330		330
Interest	20		20
Taxes	37		37
2 Other Resources Applied			
Dividends		$54	54
Fixed Assets		40	40
Total Resources Applied	$2,740	$94	$2,834
Ending Cash Balance			$ 34
Net Resources from Operations	$ (49)		
Net Resources from Management Discretion		$41	
Change in Cash Balance			$ (8)

period. Given the fact that balance sheets balance and that changes in balance sheets must therefore balance, the statement proves to the balance in the cash account at the end of the period. In a manner of speaking, since the statement appears to have more values in it and to be more complex, the fact that it begins with the cash balance at the start of the period and proves to the cash balance at the end of the period provides a fail-safe mechanism in terms of construction.

The statement of liquidity, financing, and investment activities has three columns. The first column is labeled "Operations." The values in this column are determined by comparing each income statement account with its related balance sheet account(s). For example, sales would be related to accounts and notes receivable. Cost of goods sold would be related first to purchases and then to accounts payable. Operating expenses would be related to accruals and other payables.

Recognizing that an analyst deals with information after the fact, the integration of each income statement account with its related balance sheet account(s) allows the analyst to move from accrual accounting to cash accounting. Thus, the operations column reflects the cash inflows and cash outflows and, therefore, the net cash flow of the firm. The second column is labeled management discretion. Immediately people suggest that everything within the firm is management discretion. True, but does management actively discuss every minor item at board meetings? Certainly not! In fact, at board meetings, specific types of decisions are discussed, debated, and decided on. These decisions are financing- and investment-related. It is these decisions, or their dollar values, which are typically reflected in the column labeled management discretion. From an accounting point of view, since balance sheets balance and changes to the balance sheets must therefore balance, the values shown in the management discretion column are the changes in balance sheet accounts which do not have a specific relationship to any individual income statement account.

Does this statement format conform to the three purposes of the statement of changes in financial position? Definitely! The operations column clearly reflects the cash flow position of the firm. The management discretion column reflects the financing and investment activities of the firm. The statement proves to the balance of the cash account at the end of the period. In fact, the net cash flow shown in the operations column when adjusted by the net resources for management discretion as shown in the second column, proves to the change in the cash account.

A casual observation of the information contained in Figure 5 indicates that the cash flow of the firm was indeed significantly different from the total of net income plus depreciation. In fact, the cash flow of the firm was ($49,000) while the total of net income plus depreciation was $66,000 (as shown in Figure 4). What's the difference between the two values? Obviously there is a numerical difference. More important, however, the difference can be summarized with one word: timing. In other words, the difference between the two values is the difference between accrual accounting and cash accounting. It's the difference between a funds-based concept, that is for example, the profitability of the firm as shown on the income statement versus a cash-based concept such as the net cash flow shown in the statement of liquidity, financing, and investment activities. Whereas all cash is funds but not all funds are cash, the statement of liquidity, financing, and investment activities bridges the gap, synthesizes the income statement to its respective balance sheets, and eliminates the timing differentials that a firm encounters with respect to the collection of its receivables and the payment of its payables.

One last point . . .

Does the statement of liquidity, financing, and investment activities relate at all to a cash budget? Absolutely! A cash budget simply reflects the cash inflows and cash outflows of the firm on a forecasted or before-the-fact basis. The statement of liquidity, financing, and investment activities reflects the cash inflows and cash outflows of the firm on an after-the-fact basis. In essence, our traditional modus operandi is to take the historical data of the firm and analyze it so as to establish a basis for making a financial decision which relates to the future operation of the firm.

We construct the statement of liquidity, financing, and investment activities from a historical point of view so as to gain insight on the cash flow position of the firm. Our intent is to draw inferences from the past that we can use as a basis for making a decision which extends to the future. A cash budget offers cash flow information before the fact. In other words, a cash budget is intended to be a forecast. It is typically supplied along with proforma balance sheets and income statements. If we take the time to generate a statement of liquidity, financing, and investment activities using the proforma data supplied, don't we create the opportunity to compare the cash flow forecasted through the cash budget with the cash flow of the firm as "stated" in the balance sheets and income statements? Again the answer is yes, yes indeed. The statement of liquidity, financing, and investment activities can be constructed on a historical basis or proforma basis. The information that it contains—cash flow—is too important to be ignored. □

Cash Flow from Operations and Liquidity Analysis: A New Financial Ratio for Commercial Lending Decisions

by Lyn M. Fraser

As commercial banks' credit losses continue to increase, more attention is being focused on the usefulness of traditional financial ratios in analyzing potential borrowers' financial condition. In this article, Lyn Fraser suggests a new ratio which emphasizes cash generated from operations. It is intended to supplement, rather than replace, traditional ratios.

The author is a certified public accountant and affiliated with the department of finance, Texas A&M University, College Station, Texas.

Increasing credit losses experienced by commercial banks in recent years have intensified management concerns over the loan risk evaluation and review process. Attention has focused particularly on the adequacy of the financial analysis of prospective borrowers performed by banking organizations and the usefulness of traditional financial ratios. It may be that the commonly used measures of liquidity, profitability, and leverage are no longer adequate to assess the risk dimensions of a loan. Thus it may be necessary to supplement the traditional financial ratios with others that provide more insight into the operations of the borrower. This article suggests one such supplemental ratio that appears to hold promise as an additional tool in credit analysis.

The new ratio will include as a component "cash flow from operations," an analytical tool which has gained prominence in recent years both for credit and for investment analysis.[1] The increased emphasis on cash generated from operations is particularly justified in view of the recent high levels of interest rates, which raised dramatically the cost of borrowing to cover short-term liquidity problems, and sustained inflation, which has distorted the usefulness of net income as a measure of operating performance. In fact, many of the large banking organizations now include in their spread sheet analysis either a cash basis statement of changes in financial position, showing cash generated from operations, or an income statement adjusted from an accrual to a cash basis, to reflect cash income production. The ratio presented here represents an attempt to incorporate cash flow from operations and other variables into a new financial ratio, intended primarily as a supplement to the current ratio in liquidity analysis.

How should liquidity be measured?

Any consideration of a loan request will involve an evaluation of liquidity—the ability of the borrower to generate sufficient cash to meet its cash needs, including debt service—as a critical element. Traditional discussions of financial ratios generally begin with a description of the current ratio (current assets/current liabilities) as the most commonly used measure of liquidity or at least of the short-run solvency of a business firm. In reality, the usefulness of this ratio to assess a firm's ability to cover debts as they come due is, in some cases, questionable. Does the current ratio provide this information? The current ratio is based on historical balance sheet data and relates the amount of current assets, if liquidated at stated amounts, to current liabilities on any balance sheet date. The actual value of the numerator will critically depend on the quality of its components, in particular the collectibility of accounts receivable and the salability of inventory in the future. A firm can thus have a relatively high current ratio but simultaneously low liquidity if accounts receivable are deteriorating in quality or there is a build-up of obsolete or slow-moving inventory.

Ideally, a liquidity ratio should relate future inflows of cash to future outflows of cash. While precise forecasts of these amounts are not likely, it may be possible to select historical data which are more relevant than the balance sheet current asset accounts. Specifically, cash flow from operations

---

[1] See, in particular, J. E. Perry, "Cash Flow—the Most Critical Issue of the 1980s," *The Journal of Commercial Bank Lending,* September 1982; J. E. Ketz and R. F. Kochanek, "Cash Flow: Assessing a Company's Real Financial Health," *Financial Executive,* July 1982; R. Greene, "Are More Chryslers in the Offing?," *Forbes,* February 2, 1981; J. A. Largay and C. P. Stickney, "Cash Flows, Ratio Analysis, and the W.T. Grant Bankruptcy," *Financial Analysts Journal,* July–August 1980.

(CFO) provides a measure of the amount of cash generated internally from the operations of the business during an accounting period. CFO reflects the amount of goods, services, and accounts receivable actually converted into cash. Furthermore, CFO is a more rigorous measure of funds flow than net income, cash "throw off" (net income plus depreciation), or working capital from operations. An example of the calculation should be helpful in understanding its usefulness in liquidity analysis. It should be pointed out that CFO can be calculated from any set of published financial statements and thus can be used by external as well as internal analysts.

What is cash flow from operations?

Most firms report in the statement of changes in financial position the figure "working capital from operations," which is calculated by adding back to income those deducted items which did not actually involve an outflow of working capital (such as depreciation expense and an increase in deferred tax liability). Then, those items (such as income from a subsidiary accounted for by the equity method) which contributed to net income but did not involve an inflow of working capital are subtracted. What working capital from operations does not reveal is certain items reflecting cash.

An example of CFO

For example, sales revenue generates net income, but if accounts receivable for the firm have increased over the measurement period, all of that revenue has not been collected in cash. If inventories have increased on a net basis, working capital also increases but perhaps in the form of obsolete or slow-moving inventory which cannot be readily converted to cash.

On the liability side, the firm may have increased its accounts payable to suppliers, thus reducing working capital. The purchase of goods would be reflected as an expense within cost of goods sold, but there would be no actual outflow of cash. The reverse situation would occur from a net decrease in accounts payable. The calculation of CFO takes such items into account by adjusting working capital from operations for changes in the current asset and liability accounts which affect operating income.

Consider, for example, the income statement and balance sheet situation at year-end 1982 for two firms shown in Tables 1 and 2.

Calculating CFO

To calculate CFO, start with working capital from operations and adjust for changes in the *operating* current accounts (excluding the short-term note payable because it is a "nonoperating" current account, reflecting credit from

Table 1—Income Statement for Year Ended 12/31/82

	Firm A	Firm B
Sales	$1,000,000	$1,000,000
Cost of Goods Sold	700,000	700,000
Gross Profit	300,000	300,000
Other Expense		
Selling and Administrative	120,000	90,000
Depreciation	10,000	30,000
Other	20,000	30,000
Earnings Before Tax	150,000	150,000
Income Tax Expense	75,000	75,000
Net Income	$ 75,000	$ 75,000

an external source rather than credit spontaneously generated in the course of business). To that, add decreases in current assets and increases in current liabilities and deduct increases in current assets and decreases in current liabilities, as shown in Table 3.

Both firms had sales of $1 million and net income of $75,000. Firm A generated, however, far less cash from operations than Firm B because Firm A had a

Table 2—Balance Sheet at 12/31/81 and 12/31/82

	Firm A		Firm B	
	1981	1982	1981	1982
Cash & MKT Securities	$100,000	$100,000	$100,000	$100,000
Accounts Receivable	100,000	130,000	100,000	110,000
Inventory	200,000	220,000	200,000	180,000
Total Current Assets	400,000	450,000	400,000	390,000
Property, Plant & Equipment (Net)	300,000	320,000	300,000	380,000
Total Assets	$700,000	$770,000	$700,000	$770,000
Accounts Payable	$100,000	$ 90,000	$100,000	$120,000
Accrued Expenses	100,000	110,000	100,000	110,000
Note Payable	$100,000	120,000	100,000	100,000
Total Current Liab.	300,000	320,000	300,000	330,000
Long-Term Debt	200,000	220,000	200,000	200,000
Stockholders' Equity	200,000	230,000	200,000	240,000
Total Liab. & Equity	$700,000	$770,000	$700,000	$770,000

Table 3—Cash Flow from Operations

	Firm A	Firm B
Net Income	$75,000	$75,000
+Depreciation	10,000	30,000
Working Capital From Operations	85,000	105,000
Changes in operating current accounts:		
Accounts Receivable	(30,000)	(10,000)
Inventory	(20,000)	20,000
Accounts Payable	(10,000)	20,000
Accrued Expenses	10,000	10,000
Cash Flow From Operations	$35,000	$145,000

greater buildup of accounts receivable, an increase in inventory, and a net retirement of payables to suppliers. Firm B internally generated more cash than Firm A, but its current ratio actually declined from 1.33 to 1.18 while Firm A had an increase in its current ratio from 1.33 to 1.41. Which firm is more liquid? It is difficult to determine. Firm A has a higher current ratio because of the increase in inventories and receivables. The question is, can they be converted into cash at the stated balance sheet amounts? In 1982, Firm B has demonstrated a greater ability to turn sales dollars into cash.

A new liquidity ratio

The purpose of this article is to develop a new measure of liquidity which would incorporate CFO with a firm's liquid current assets. The new ratio would be:

$$\frac{\text{CFO} + \text{Cash Assets (Cash and Marketable Securities)}}{\text{Current Liabilities}}$$

Is this a viable ratio? The numerator immediately presents a problem because it mixes a flow (CFO) and a stock (cash assets). Furthermore, CFO is actually a source of cash, so adding CFO to cash assets would appear to be double-counting. Finally, the new ratio still uses historical data to predict uncertain future flows.

Consider, however, the proposal from another perspective. What a liquidity ratio attempts to measure is the ability of a firm to generate cash to meet cash needs. Cash and marketable securities are liquid current assets, a ready source of cash. CFO reflects the ability of the firm to generate cash internally, from the operations of the business. CFO could be viewed as a substitute for inventory and accounts receivable in the existing current ratio, as a proxy for the ability of the firm to translate inventory and accounts receivable into cash. And it is cash which the firm needs to pay debts. The stock (cash assets), then, is actually a real source of future cash. The flow (CFO) is added to the real stock of cash as a measure of how much additional cash will be available from selling inventory and collecting from customers. CFO is historical data, but it does reflect real cash generation and, therefore, should be useful in liquidity measurement.

Interpreting the ratio

In the example on page 49, if the new ratio were used, the two firms would have short-term liquidity ratios in 1982 as follows:

$$\frac{\text{CFO + Cash Assets}}{\text{Current Liabilities}} \qquad \textbf{Firm A}\quad \frac{35{,}000 + 100{,}000}{320{,}000} = .42 \qquad \textbf{Firm B}\quad \frac{145{,}000 + 100{,}000}{330{,}000} = .74$$

It would appear that Firm B is the more liquid of the two, reflecting a greater generation of internal cash.

As with any financial ratio, these should be interpreted with caution. First, we are lacking any data on the trends of the two firms. Second, the above ratios should be compared with industry standards. Finally, and perhaps most important, the causes of the higher CFO for Firm B should be explored and explained.

The above ratio could be expanded if desired, depending on the firm's method of financing and the perspective of the analyst, to include all liabilities in the denominator:

$$\frac{\text{CFO + Cash Assets}}{\text{Total Liabilities}} \qquad \textbf{Firm A}\quad \frac{35{,}000 + 100{,}000}{540{,}000} = .25 \qquad \textbf{Firm B}\quad \frac{145{,}000 + 100{,}000}{530{,}000} = .46$$

These calculations would again favor Firm B, which has apparently been able to finance its expansion of property, plant, and equipment internally.

Examples

Two food industry companies

The new ratio using CFO would be particularly useful for retail, wholesale, and manufacturing firms which carry proportionately large amounts of inven-

Table 4—CFO Ratio Compared to Current Ratio

Anderson, Clayton & Co.		**1980**	**1981**	**1982**
Current assets	($mil.)	$552.8	$535.1	$549.0
Current liab.	($mil.)	$311.4	$301.5	$269.7
Current ratio		1.77	1.77	2.04
Cash assets	($mil.)	$122.5	$136.1	$190.7
CFO	($mil.)	$ (10.3)	$125.7	$100.4
CFO + Cash assets/Cur. liab.		.36	.87	1.08
Sysco Corp.		**1980**	**1981**	**1982**
Current assets	($mil.)	$197.7	$240.5	$305.4
Current liab.	($mil.)	$ 99.7	$121.7	$155.3
Current ratio		1.98	1.98	1.97
Cash assets	($mil.)	$ 39.2	$ 56.1	$ 50.6
CFO	($mil.)	$ 42.8	$ 35.7	$ 31.9
CFO + Cash assets/Cur. liab.		.82	.75	.53

tories and receivables and which finance working capital, in part, through trade payables. These are the types of business firms for which CFO is especially critical. An examination was made of two companies—Anderson, Clayton & Co. and Sysco Corp.—over a three-year period (1980–1982)[2] to determine what might be revealed by using the new ratio compared to the current ratio to measure liquidity (see Table 4). Both companies operate in various aspects of the wholesale food industry. Anderson, Clayton & Co. is primarily engaged in food processing and animal foods; Sysco Corp. is mainly a food distributor to restaurants and institutions.

Without complete underlying data, it is not possible to perform a thorough liquidity analysis of the two firms. The objective, rather, is to use the new liquidity ratio to reveal additional information about each firm's short-term liquidity position. Looking at the current ratio first, it would appear that Anderson, Clayton experienced an improvement in short-term liquidity for fiscal 1982 compared to 1980 and 1981, when the current ratio was constant. Sysco's current ratio is stable over the three-year period at a level of 2.0.

Using the new ratio

The new ratio (CFO + Cash assets/Current liabilities) reveals a somewhat different picture. Anderson, Clayton steadily improved its short-term liquidity

[2] Data used are for *fiscal* years ending in 1980, 1981, and 1982. The fiscal year for Anderson Clayton & Co. ended on June 30 for each year; the fiscal year for Sysco Corp. ended on June 28, 1980; June 27, 1981; and July 3, 1982.

as a result of turning around a negative CFO in 1980 to a strongly positive internal generation of cash in 1981 and 1982. Anderson, Clayton also increased its holdings of cash assets and reduced current liabilities over the period. Sysco Corp., which is a growth company, has almost the reverse experience. CFO, while positive, has been declining, and current liabilities have increased sharply. The result is an apparent deterioration in liquidity as measured by the new ratio. While some decline in liquidity may not prove to be a serious problem for a growth firm with strong earnings and positive cash flow, the analyst should be alert to a potential weakness in liquidity and should explore the causes.

Conclusion

The proposed new ratio will not provide definitive conclusions about a firm's liquidity position; nor will it satisfy the theoreticians. Rather, the development of a liquidity ratio which includes cash flow from operations represents an effort to add a new liquidity ratio to the stock of analytical tools enabling analysts to relate inflows and outflows of funds. The actual usefulness of the new ratio can best be determined by its application in liquidity analysis for credit and investment decisions, particularly for firms which carry relatively large amounts of inventories and receivables. For these firms, a buildup of inventories and receivables could result in an increasing current ratio which is misleading if these assets cannot be converted into cash. Further, the usefulness of the ratio can be extended to consider the financing patterns of particular firms. For a firm which finances with long-term debt, an additional ratio or ratios should be calculated to include total liabilities or current liabilities plus long-term debt in the denominator. □

Analyzing the Quantity and Quality of Cash Flow for Long-Term Borrowing

by Dev Strischek

Both quantitative and qualitative considerations are important in term loan cash flow analysis. In the following article, Dev Strischek discusses five different ratios for evaluating a firm's solvency position. In his opinion, the major problem in using these types of ratios is how to compare tax-deductible expenses with nondeductible funds outlays. The five ratio formulas he presents all allow for making this comparison.

The importance of earnings quality becomes author Strischek's focus in the latter part of the article as he demonstrates how various accounting practices can distort the earnings picture.

The author is senior vice president, credit services, Barnett Bank of Palm Beach County, Palm Beach, Florida. At the time this article was first published in May 1980, he was vice president, Commerce Bank of Kansas City, N.A., Kansas City, Missouri.

As commercial borrowers' needs have become more complex, bankers have had to extend their time horizons for debt repayment. It used to be that seasonal lenders presumed repayment to flow from the current assets' cash cycle. But today's commercial lenders increasingly must deal with firms whose borrowings must be repaid from cash flow.

Our national obsession with growth, for better or for worse, permeates our business community and is reflected in decisions stressing revenue and profit expansion. This expansion, in turn, requires increases in minimum levels of working capital and fixed assets. Earnings cannot completely fund the desired growth, and the equity markets have never been accessible to most of America's corporate borrowers.

A number of financial institutions have risen to the challenge. Insurance companies, finance companies, and investment firms have been long-term lenders for years; it is the commercial banking industry that has been the laggard in term lending. The trend from lines of credit to revolvers to outright term loans is clear to any observer of credit markets. The task before bankers is to develop the quantitative and qualitative tools necessary to assess the volume, stability, and quality of cash flow.

Reasons for long-term borrowing

A basic tenet of finance is that short-term assets should be financed with short-term debt and long-term assets with long-term debt and equity. In other words, we fund the uses with sources of equal duration.

The typical reasons for long-term borrowing, then, are generally uses associated with sales and operations expansion such as:

(1) An increase in noncurrent assets, usually new fixed assets.

(2) An increase in the minimum or permanent net working capital levels.

(3) Repayment of long-term debt.

Repayment obligations

Ultimately, the lender expects that earnings from operations will fund these uses because the primary purpose of the expansion is to generate profits. If there are no profits to be made, there is no reason to expand. Economists are very quick to tell us that we only increase production as long as the extra costs required to expand are covered by extra profits; economists say that when marginal profits equal marginal costs, the firm is maximizing its profits.

Permanent current assets and liabilities

Creditors and, in turn, owners commit funds to a firm with the reasonable expectation that the firm will repay loans plus a fair rate of interest to the creditors and will declare satisfactory dividends for the shareholders. Moreover, the firm has internal financial responsibilities to maintain its productive assets at optimal efficiency.

While the term "permanent assets" is primarily restricted to capital assets and other noncurrent assets, it should also be recognized that the firm must carry a minimum level of current assets. This minimum level is properly part of the permanent assets, and that portion of current liabilities carried year around should be considered permanent debt. These permanent current assets and liabilities do not have directly associated servicing requirements. But their expansion and contraction should theoretically be funded through corresponding changes in debtors' equity, that is, by liabilities and owners' equity.

Firm's ability to service six primary obligations

Being able to service its obligations means the firm is able to pay interest expense on outstanding debt, meet the debt repayment as scheduled, pay adequate preferred and common stock dividends, and set aside a portion of earnings through depreciation and amortization to replenish the firm's productive assets. In addition, where leased facilities and equipment are a significant proportion of productive assets, the lease expense's fixed contractual payment is a relevant factor in appraising the firm's ability to service its permanent obligations. These six outlays—interest expense, debt repayment, preferred dividends, common dividends, capital expenditures, and lease expense—are the principal uses of funds generated by operations. A firm unable to fund its permanent obligations will be unable to maintain its assets. One definition of solvency is the ability of a firm to repay its long-term obligations.

We can quantitatively judge a firm's solvency through ratios comparing various sources of funds with various uses.

Introduction to solvency ratios

There are several ratios by which to judge a firm's solvency position, but they all share the same approach. Earnings and/or cash flow (earnings plus depreciation) are compared to various expenses and outlays associated with a firm's permanent debt, owner's equity, and permanent assets. The funds available for paying the various outlays are usually divided by the outlays; thus, the higher the ratio, the better is the coverage of the outlays by the funds from operations. A ratio of less than 1.00 means that, within the context of the ratio, funds from operations are less than outlays being compared. Therefore, the coverage as defined by that ratio is inadequate.

Before-tax outlays vs. after-tax outlays

The major problem in using solvency ratios is how to compare tax-deductible expenses with nondeductible outlays. Under corporate tax laws, lease payments, interest, and depreciation are deductible expenses; however, dividends, debt repayments, and capital expenditures are not tax-deductible. Therefore, nondeductible outlays require a greater before-tax portion of earnings than the tax-deductible expenses.

For example, a $5 common stock dividend declared by a company in a 48% corporate income tax bracket has to earn $9.62 in order to have a sum after taxes equal to the declared dividend:

$$\begin{bmatrix}\text{Earnings before}\\ \text{taxes required}\\ \text{to pay a \$5.00}\\ \text{dividend}\end{bmatrix} \times \begin{bmatrix}\text{1–48\% income}\\ \text{tax}\end{bmatrix} = \text{\$5.00 dividend after taxes}$$

$$\begin{bmatrix}\text{Earnings before}\\ \text{taxes required}\\ \text{to pay a \$5.00}\\ \text{dividend}\end{bmatrix} = \frac{\text{\$5.00 div. A. T.}}{(1.00 - .48)}$$

$$\begin{bmatrix}\text{Earnings before}\\ \text{taxes required}\\ \text{to pay a \$5.00}\\ \text{dividend after}\\ \text{taxes}\end{bmatrix} = \text{\$9.62}$$

It is clear from this example that the corporate income tax rate distorts and consequently precludes logical comparison of tax-deductible expenses with after-tax nondeductible outlays. Meaningful analysis is possible only if the data are comparable. Hence, one outlay must be converted to the tax position of the other.

The preferred approach is to convert nondeductible outlays to their pre-tax earnings equivalent. A before-tax basis eliminates the difference in the tax rate often encountered in comparative analysis of small and large companies. Moreover, even internal analysis is affected by the year-to-year differences in corporate profits and the concomitant income tax rate.

Simple formula

The formula for converting after-tax amounts to before-tax amounts can be stated in shortened form as follows:

$$\textbf{(Before \$)}\ (1.00 - r) = \textbf{(After \$)}$$

$$\textbf{(Before \$)} = \frac{\textbf{(After \$)}}{(1.00 - r)}$$

The logical proof behind the formula was presented in the $5 dividend example. Here it is again stated in the shortened form just given:

$$\textbf{(Before \$)}\ (1.00 - r) = \textbf{(After \$)}$$

$$\textbf{(Before \$)}\ (1.00 - .48) = \$5.00$$

$$\textbf{(Before \$)} = \frac{\$5.00}{(1.00 - .48)} = \frac{\$5.00}{.52} = \$9.62$$

Solvency ratios

With the mechanics of the solvency ratios perfected, the solvency ratios per se can now be discussed. Each of the following five ratios has its strengths and weaknesses, but all five conform to the general principles and quantitative mechanics presented in this section.

Times-interest-earned ratio

One of the most widely used solvency ratios is the times-interest-earned ratio. The increased use of long-term debt, its senior position over owners' equity in the capital structure, and the resultant practice of highlighting interest expense in financial statements make this aspect of solvency appraisal hard to ignore and easy to calculate.

Both long-term creditors and owners concentrate attention on the portion of the earnings stream to which they are entitled. But present and prospective long-term creditors examine the operating statement to see how adequately their interest return is covered by the pre-tax operating income. Bondholders, banks, insurance companies, and other long-term creditors usually enjoy a variety of protective convenants. Such covenants ensure that the debt will be repaid at the promised time and compensate the lender for the use of his money by the payment of an interest charge. A breach or violation of a covenant usually gives the lender the right to accelerate the date of maturity or some other privilege unfavorable to the debtor. In view of these undesirable remedies, the analyst may sensibly assume that at least one basic solvency guideline is the ability of a firm to cover its interest expense at least once.

The times-interest-earned ratio is calculated as follows:

$$\text{Times-interest-earned} = \frac{\text{EBIT}}{\text{Interest expense}}$$

where EBIT equals earnings before interest and taxes.

A minimum solvency guideline of 1.00 more was suggested earlier. However, a typical guideline is 3.00 to 8.00 because of the variations in earnings and interest expense from period to period and also because of differences between various lines of business. For the sake of comparison, Moody's and Standard and Poor's bond ratings of top rated Aaa/AAA industrial companies show a 16.84 average, and their medium grade industrial companies, a 4.21 average coverage for the 1973–1978 period.

Fixed charges coverage ratio

Besides applying funds to the payment of interest expense on its long-term debt, a firm must also commit funds to repayment of the debt principal. Scheduled repayments of principal are just as mandatory as interest payments. Any failure to pay according to the debt agreement would normally subject the firm to the same unfavorable circumstances as encountered in default on the interest expense. Although scheduled debt repayments can be delayed, they inevitably must be repaid. A conservative analytical approach is to assume that the debt will be repaid as agreed. Scheduled debt repayment is equally as important in appraising a firm's solvency as is the interest expense factor.

Debt repayment is the reduction of a liability and therefore cannot be considered a cost of doing business any more than the original proceeds of the loan can be counted as income. In a sense, a portion of the earnings must be retained in the business to repay debt. Debt repayment is not tax-deductible and must be converted to its pre-tax earnings equivalent to use it in this ratio.

Current maturities of long-term debt. For practical purposes, the balance sheet item shown as "current maturities of long-term debt" under the current liabilities classification is satisfactory for use as the scheduled debt repayment. The desired approach is to match the scheduled debt repayment of the previous accounting period with the outlays of the present period—the period during which the debt repayment would presumably occur. If this approach is impractical, then the current period's long-term debt maturities is acceptable provided that this amount is applied consistently in all the ratios and throughout the trend series.

Preferred dividend. A second outlay that tacitly functions as a fixed burden is the preferred dividend. Theoretically, the preferred stock combines the limited obligation of a bond with the flexibility of common stock. In exchange for his first claim to dividends, the preferred stockholder's priority in dividends is generally limited to a fixed percentage of the par value of the stock or a fixed number of dollars per share for no par stock. However, the security of his preferred position is usually reinforced with the "cumulative" feature; before any common dividend can be paid, not only must the current preferred stock be paid but also any unpaid preferred dividends declared in previous years.

The prior claim of the preferred stockholder does not guarantee a fixed, regular rate of return. The claim only establishes an order of priority by which the board of directors will pay dividends if it decides to declare dividends at all. The fixed nature of the claim sets a definite upper limit to the preferred shareholders' claims on earnings. The prior position of preferred stock also usually extends to the disposition of assets in event of liquidation but only with respect to common stock. The senior position of creditors remains unaffected.

The pressure for a regular, consistent common dividend record virtually assures the preferred dividend's prior claim on dividends as a fixed burden. The common stock's market performance is not enhanced by a history of unpaid preferred dividends. If a firm cannot effectively compete in the equity capital market for additional funds with new common stock offerings, management inevitably treats the preferred stock as if it were a bond issue and regularly pays the full preferred dividend.

Tax laws interpret preferred dividends as a distribution of net profits to owners rather than as a business cost. Thus, preferred dividends must be converted to the pre-tax earnings equivalent to be on the same basis as interest expense.

Lease expense. A third item that should be included in the fixed charge coverage is lease expense. FASB 13 and its amendments have essentially eliminated off-balance sheet financing by promulgating the concepts of capital leases and operating leases. A capital lease asset is capitalized and its obligation recorded as a liability. Operating leases are still expensed and are the obligation under discussion in this paragraph. Capital lease repayment is a long-term debt reduction, and if the firm could not pay the rent on its leased productive assets—facilities and equipment—the company could not continue operations. While this argument could conceivably be extended to other operating expenses, lease expense is exceptional in that it is usually contractually fixed at an agreed-upon sum over a period of time. Lease expense essentially functions similarly to debt repayment and is in fact the servicing of an obligation, capitalized or not.

Since lease expense is recognized as a legitimate business expense, it is directly comparable with interest expense. No conversion to a pre-tax basis is necessary because lease expense is already on a before-tax basis.

The fixed charges coverage ratio is simply the times-interest-earned ratio expanded to include lease expense, debt repayment, and preferred dividends compared to earnings, all on a pre-tax basis:

$$\text{Fixed charges coverage} = \frac{\text{EBIT + lease expense}}{\text{Interest exp.} + \text{Lease exp.} + \dfrac{\text{Preferred Dividends}}{(1.00 - r)} + \dfrac{\text{Scheduled Dbt. Repay.}}{(1.00 - r)}}$$

Obviously, the fixed charges coverage ratio shows a lower quantitative coverage than does the times-interest-earned ratio. This lower coverage is due to the inclusion of more factors in the solvency appraisal. The lower ratio is probably a better indicator of the solvency position than simply the times-interest-earned ratio.

Debt repayment coverage ratio

This ratio is one of few solvency ratios published among industry statistics; it is calculated and printed in RMA's *Annual Statement Studies*.[1]

The debt repayment coverage ratio compares cash flow to current maturities of long-term debt:

$$\text{Debt repayment coverage ratio} = \frac{\text{Net profit after taxes} + \text{depreciation}}{\text{Scheduled debt repayment}}$$

Cash flow or "throw-off" is the primary source of regular long-term debt repayment, and this ratio purportedly measures the cash flow coverage of such debt service. However, the two components of cash flow, depreciation and earnings, have other uses. Depreciation expense is ideally reserved for fixed asset replacement, and a portion of net profits is supposed to pay dividends. Nevertheless, cash flow is also the primary source of funds for repayment of debt.

The debt repayment coverage ratio lacks the detailed analytical scope of the fixed charges coverage ratio, matches debt repayment with the inappropriate operating period, and assumes that earnings plus depreciation represents the true cash flow. Nevertheless, this ratio does provide a rough approximation of the firm's ability to retire debt each year from cash generated by operations. Both cash flow and scheduled debt repayment are on an after-tax basis which eliminates the necessity of pre-tax conversion. Although depreciation expense is a tax-deductible expense, it is also a noncash consuming expense. Thus, the full portion of revenues reduced by depreciation is additional cash earnings theoretically available for capital expenditures. However, inflation has rendered depreciation reserves practically useless as the sole source of funds for capital asset replacement. *Value Line* recently reported that depreciation expense covered only 68% of the estimated replacement cost of productive capacity in 1978 for 175 companies in 14 industries.

Comparison with industry statistics, such as RMA's *Statement Studies*, would provide a guideline for judging the adequacy or inadequacy of the quantitative values of these ratios.

---

[1] Published annually. Available from RMA, 1616 Philadelphia National Bank Building, Philadelphia, PA 19107. Contact RMA for pricing information.

Debt and capital expenditures coverage ratio

The addition of capital expenditures to the scheduled debt repayment to be covered by cash flow yields a ratio employed by the bond rating services in evaluating public offerings:

$$\text{Debt \& capital expenditures coverage} = \frac{\text{Net profit after taxes} + \text{depreciation}}{\text{Scheduled debt repayment} + \text{Capital expenditures}}$$

The major rating services consider .5 to be acceptable for this ratio. Here we have combined two major uses of funds and compared them to the available cash flow. A norm of 50% suggests that the average industrial firm can only rely on its internal cash flow for 50% of the funds needed to add new plant and repay old debt.

Both the debt repayment coverage ratio and the debt and capital expenditures coverage ratio are relatively easy to compute because of their after-tax position. Both ratios also have limited industry statistical data for external comparative analysis. Unfortunately, neither ratio recognizes the pre-tax burdens of interest, lease expense, and dividends on cash flow.

Funds flow ratio

The funds flow ratio is an attempt to consolidate the conceptual advantages of all the preceding ratios into one ratio. The ratio comprises the six major outlays—interest expense, lease expense, scheduled debt repayment, preferred dividends, common dividends, and capital expenditures—on a pre-tax basis compared to the corresponding pre-tax cash flow. The only component not in the other four ratios is common dividends.

Common dividends are not an enforceable commitment, but common stockholders have residual equity. They are entitled to consider as theirs all earnings after prior charges whether or not distributed as dividends. Moreover, in the discussion of preferred dividends, it was stressed that a company seeking additional equity from time to time is obliged to maintain a fairly regular dividend policy on both classes of stock.

The funds flow associated with common dividends must be converted to the pre-tax earnings equivalent because the law does not permit common dividends to be considered a cost of business.

The funds flow coverage ratio formula is shown below:

$$\text{Funds Flow Coverage} = \frac{\text{EBIT} + \text{Lease expense} + \text{Depreciation expense}}{\text{Int. Exp.} + \text{Lease Exp.} + \dfrac{\text{Sched. Dbt. Repay.} + \text{Pref. Div.} + \text{Common Div.} + \text{Capital Expend.}}{(1.00 - r)}}$$

The lack of industry statistics precludes external comparative analysis, as is the case with three of the other four ratios. As a tool for internal analysis, the funds flow coverage ratio summarizes the trends reflected in the other four ratios for measuring the quantity of cash flow available for the six major outlays.

Systematic calculation of the solvency ratios

The data to calculate the ratios should be organized in logical order and the ratios themselves should be arranged so that they reflect more and more obligations to cover. If so done, the computation and interpretation of the ratios will be simpler and easier to understand.

Hypothetical data for Nationwide Airlines, a fictitious national airline, is presented below. Note its poor performance in 1974 and 1975 and its general recovery after 1975.

		For the year ended 12/31:				
Given and Expressed in $MM		**1974**	**1975**	**1976**	**1977**	**1978**
1. Interest expense		63.9	67.2	64.7	90.4	79.4
2. Lease expense		152.3	162.5	167.4	87.2	97.7
3. Debt repayment		67.2	93.5	49.3	120.2	97.5
4. Preferred dividends		1.0	-0-	-0-	1.0	1.0
5. Common dividends		1.1	-0-	-0-	9.3	10.6
6. Capital expenditures		216.7	106.4	98.1	97.7	190.2
7. Federal income taxes		.8	(17.2)	25.3	16.0	5.9
8. Profit after taxes		(23.6)	(86.3)	36.8	64.8	86.6
9. Depreciation expense		122.2	128.2	130.5	133.5	190.8
Calculated and Expressed as ( )						
10. Tax rate (r)	(%)	3.3	(16.0)	40.7	19.8	6.4
11. Cash flow	($MM)	98.6	41.9	167.3	198.3	177.4
12. EBIT	(X)	41.1	(36.3)	126.8	171.2	171.9
13. Times interest earned	(X)	.64	(.54)	1.96	1.81	2.16
14. Fixed charges coverage	(X)	.71	.41	.75	1.04	.88
15. Debt repayment coverage	(X)	1.47	.47	3.39	2.01	2.85
16. Debt & cptl expenditures cov.	(X)	.35	.21	1.14	.91	.46
17. Funds flow coverage	(X)	.61	.68	.83	.81	.91

Interest coverage has generally increased since the 1975 loss year. The fixed charge coverage ratio and the debt and capital expenditure ratio fell in 1978 because of the heavier capital expenditures. The funds flow ratio was not so affected because capital expenditures were tax-factored and debt repayment was lower. Since the funds flow ratio is the most inclusive of the group, the overall trend seems to be one of the generally increasing coverage.

Summary of quantitative analysis

Five ratios have been offered and explained for use in determining a firm's solvency position. All five are mechanically similar in that earnings and/or cash flow available to pay certain outlays are compared to the various outlays. The individual differences in the ratios are the result of the outlays considered and their tax position in relation to the funds flow available to cover them. Industry statistics are relatively scarce, so external comparative analysis is limited for the most part. However, the five ratios do provide a good base of data for internal solvency trend analysis.

This discussion of solvency analysis has been limited to a historical approach. That is, past results have been assumed to be a reasonable basis for predicting the firm's present and future solvency position. Indeed, this is an implicit assumption in all trend analysis. Nevertheless, we still need reasonably formulated projections of earnings, debt repayment schedules, capital expenditures, and dividends to derive a balanced appraisal of a firm's probable future solvency.

At best, the techniques discussed in the preceding pages provide data for a static appraisal of solvency in the current time period. At the worst, these ratios may not be inclusive enough to reflect the firm's solvency position. The ratios give only quantitative values of various relationships. The qualitative appraisal of the firm's solvency requires a closer look at the rules of generally accepted accounting.

Qualitative considerations

We have assumed that the quality of earnings is not strained, or less poetically, is solid 100% cash. In fact, there are some accounting practices which can lead to considerable differences in the quality of cash flow between two companies with the very same dollar cash flow.

Earnings quality is appraised by an evaluation of a company's accounting practices. The more conservative a company's reporting methods are within generally accepted accounting principles (GAAP)—that is, the more likely the company is to minimize reported profits regardless of the level of underlying earning power—the higher will be the quality of reported earnings. Companies that use accounting techniques designed to increase reported earnings have low quality cash flow.

The conglomerate excesses of the '60s resulted in a revived awareness of how profits can be a function of accounting ingenuity rather than solid business success. The accounting profession, federal regulators, corporate officers, investment bankers, and securities analysts all became aware of the need to curb accounting gimmickry and illusions once the '60s' bubble burst. The accounting profession's AICPA and FASB and the SEC deserve praise for bold measures such as the Accounting Principles Board Opinion No. 15: Earnings per Share (APB Opinion No. 15). APB No. 15 was designed to compel more complete corporate disclosure and assist investors in pinning down earnings.

Earnings quality is very much related to balance sheet quality and overall corporate financial strength. It is possible for a troubled company to report a quality income figure. However, it is not likely that a corporation with a poor profit quality will have a high-quality balance sheet because individual accounting practices generally affect both the income statement and the balance sheet. Evaluation of earnings quality or inferiority, therefore, is a way to understand the overall soundness of a company's financial statements and a way to analyze the conservative or liberal nature of accounting practices employed in drawing up the statements.

LIFO vs. FIFO

The LIFO (last in, first out) inventory accounting method signals higher earnings quality than FIFO (first in, first out) when prices are rising because reported profits under LIFO are minimized by the higher current costing of inventory used to calculate the cost of goods sold. However, accumulating LIFO inventory profits may reflect a change in conditions warranting a reconsideration of the inventory method. For instance, during a depression when prices are supposed to be falling, FIFO would be the better method.

Accelerated depreciation vs. straight-line depreciation

Accelerated depreciation accounting for stockholder reporting purposes is preferred over the straight-line method because accelerated depreciation puts aside more funds for plant replacement and simultaneously reduces reported earnings. Depreciation has traditionally been considered part of cash flow because it is a noncash-using expense charged to operations. Any method which increases depreciation expense also increases cash flow, and since accelerated depreciation charges more depreciation to operations than straight-line depreciation in the early years of an asset's useful life, accelerated depreciation results in more cash flow as well as a lower income tax liability because of the lower earnings. However, keep in mind that when a company stops growing and depreciation booked on an accelerated basis slips below straight-line depreciation, the method is no longer so conservative.

Income deferral

It is also better to defer income while flowing through expenses within the framework of GAAP. Therefore, when a company defers a chunk of plant start-up costs, the reported profit is probably overstated. However, when it defers the benefits of, say, investment tax credits, profits are probably understated.

Tax rate

Companies which employ flow-through accounting methods and generate timing differences in financial reporting and tax reporting are likely to show low tax rates. Companies with higher, more normal income tax rates in the 45% to 50% range are likely to have better quality earnings.[2] Investment credits, capital gains tax rates, and percentage depletion allowances are vulnerable to changes in tax laws. Companies that base their profit strategies on the permanence of these tax reducers will find themselves only dependent on what may be at best a temporary and variable source of funds.

For example, the investment tax credit was introduced in 1962, was suspended for a period of time, and then increased sharply. The investment tax credit may be subject to reduction or elimination, however, because of its controversial political status, its use as a counter-cyclical incentive for investment, and the need for a sustained level of capital expenditures each year. Capital-intensive industries benefit most from the investment tax credit, and they are also sensitive to business cycles. It is not hard to imagine the Congress' indifferent attitude toward auto makers' pleas for bigger tax credits in the third or fourth year of an expansion phase of a business cycle.

Likewise, the capital gains tax feature and the percentage depletion deductions have come under increasing political pressure as tax shelters for already profitable big business. The high profits of oil companies in 1979 have not made depletion popular among individual taxpayers or some members of Congress. What is particularly appealing or appalling, depending on one's political and economic philosophy, is that the percentage depletion deductions for natural resource exploitation can cause the tax return deduction for depletion to exceed permanently the book depletion deduction and create a permanent differ-

---

[2] A certain irony would seem to exist here. While the author identifies a 45% to 50% tax bracket as high quality, he also judges cash flow to be high quality when accelerated depreciation and quick write-offs are used. However, faster write-offs would seem to reduce earnings and therefore possibly reduce the company's tax bracket.—Ed.

ence between book and tax return income. Thus, oil companies and lumber companies will carry deferred tax liabilities which will never have to be repaid—unless the law changes. And the law could change if these permanently deferred liabilities become too large and too publicized to ignore.

Full consolidation

Fully consolidated reports that assume a parent company and its subsidiaries are a single entity usually make analysis easier and eliminate intercompany sales and profits. It is important, however, to know also what part of the subsidiaries' incomes can be used by the parent for corporate purposes and dividend payments.

Summary of how accounting practices can distort earnings

There are several common accounting practices which may distort a firm's earnings, that is, understate or overstate earnings. A banker should view an understated cash flow as conservative and as affording a margin of protection for repayment of his credit. Conversely, overstated earnings lead to undue optimism and great expectations by unwary lenders. These accounting practices are summarized below in terms of understating or overstating cash flow.

	Cash flow quality	
Qualitative aspect	**High quality**	**Low quality**
1. Inventory valuation	LIFO understates profits in inflationary period	FIFO overstates profits in inflationary period
2. Depreciation method	Accelerated depreciation more accurately matches replacement cost	Straight-line depreciation under-reserves funds for fixed assets replacement; thus, it overstates earnings
3. Deferred assets	Intangibles are written off as quickly as possible	Expenses are capitalized and earnings are overstated
4. Deferred income	Income is deferred while expenses are flowed through; for example, benefits of investment tax credits are deferred	Expenses are deferred; for example, plant start-up costs and tax credits are taken immediately

Qualitative aspect	Cash flow quality: High quality	Low quality
5. Tax rate	"Normal" effective tax rate, such as 45% to 50%, usually reflects minimal reliance on various tax deferral methods—investment tax credits, capital gains credits, and percentage depletion deductions—and therefore, better quality	Low effective tax rate, such as below 40%, usually reflects reliance on various tax deferral methods which may be vulnerable to reduction or elimination; the lower effective rate suggests low quality because of the potential for change in the tax deferral methods.

Therefore, if you must choose between two borrowers with an equal earnings of say, $100,000, pick the one that values its inventory on a LIFO basis, accelerates its depreciation, amortizes its intangibles as quickly as possible, defers income, and carries the higher tax rate.

Conclusion

Cash flow is the pool of funds available for preferred and common dividends, capital expenditures, and debt repayment. We must expand the concept to a before-tax basis to recognize tax-deductible costs associated with servicing a firm's permanent obligations—that is, interest expense and lease expense. To ignore any of these uses, before-tax or after-tax, is to overestimate cash flow available for debt repayment. Prudent banking dictates appraising *all* the uses which a pool of funds is expected to service. Attempts to maximize cash flow to rationalize a marginal credit risk invites delinquencies, losses, and write-offs.

Next, the firm's accounting practices must be reviewed. Earnings are probably overstated where there is FIFO inventory valuation, straight-line depreciation, slow intangible asset amortization, immediate income recognition, and unusually low income tax rates.

If bankers are to be good term lenders, they must be able to quantitatively and qualitatively analyze a firm's cash flow and solvency. I hope this article provides a method of performing this dual analysis. □

Author's update

Subsequent to the publication of this article, income tax rates have been modified, and it is likely that these rates will be changed from time to time. Therefore, what constitutes a normal tax rate should be evaluated in the context of the prevailing incremental tax rate schedule.

The Recession-Sensitive Borrower: Evaluating Cash Flow and Financial Structure

by John R. Carter

Even though we are digging out of a recession, a borrower may submit financial statements representing periods of decreased product demand. Current statements exhibiting increased demand may also be presented. The analysis of financial statements by a lender should include an assessment of how well the operations of a company are managed during periods of recession or expansion.

In the following article, a format of cash flow analysis is presented whereby the lender can judge how efficiently assets and liabilities are managed in response to changes in revenue levels. Through the internal cash generation formula described, a lender can quickly test the logic of a company's projections for future requirements of external funds under varying conditions of demand and profitability.

The author is credit examiner, Zions First National Bank, Salt Lake City, Utah. In July 1983, when this article was originally published, he was a financial analyst with REDEX, Inc., Salt Lake City.

Without consulting a single economic index or hearing a defending argument of a political advisor, commercial lenders can detect a recession by observing the financial statements of many of their own borrowing customers. A decline in sales and other complications related either directly or indirectly to the recessionary period work to hinder profitable operations of recession-sensitive firms.

During periods of economic expansion, a company's management may recognize the need for continued growth to hold a profitable position in the marketplace. A lender would be concerned about how much growth could be sustained by the profits of the company without deteriorating the capital structure. Plagued by decreased product demand, however, the firm often becomes a victim of the economic environment and reacts in any way necessary to maintain a profitable position.

Analyzing the financial statements of a recession-sensitive firm

As a loan officer or analyst monitors the profitability or financial structure of any borrowing customer, the primary sources of information are, of course, the income statement and the balance sheet. The income statement is a summary of the dynamics of the firm and arrives at the bottom line of net profit. Spreading the statements provides insight into various operational trends. A spread of the balance sheets portrays the firm in a stop-action sense and allows a quick assessment of the changes in financial structure from year to year.

Because an expanding firm requires additional assets in support of additional sales, an analysis of where cash resources originate and for which asset increases cash is provided, gives a dynamic element to the balance sheet. A company with declining sales normally exhibits an accompanying decrease in assets. The funds provided by contracting assets should be accounted for by proper analysis to make sure the most important and critical cash needs of the firm are met.

ABC Furniture Company

The ABC Company is a wholesaler of good quality furniture which experienced sales decreases of 16.3% in 1980 and 23.7% in 1981. Assets decreased 2.5% in 1980 and 15.3% in 1981.

The financial spread of the ABC Company in Figure 1 shows that notes payable to the bank are increasing even though total assets are decreasing and that owners' equity is continuing to support over half of total assets. Accounts payable as a percent of total assets is decreasing steadily, as is the level of accounts receivable. Trends in profitability look serious, since net profit has dropped from $110,000 in 1979 to a $160,000 loss in 1981. Increasing operating expenses is the primary cause of the negative profitability trend.

Obviously, the bottom line is not the whole story. The declining assets and liabilities represent a combined result of operations, management decisions,

Figure 1—ABC Furniture Company
(Dollars in thousands)

	1979	%	1980	%	1981	%
Cash	10	.5	5	.3	5	.3
Accounts receivable	560	27.9	470	24.0	360	21.7
Inventory	1,170	58.2	1,240	63.2	1,050	63.3
Fixed assets (net)	270	13.4	245	12.5	245	14.7
Total assets	2,010	100.0	1,960	100.0	1,660	100.0
Notes payable	230	11.4	290	14.8	310	18.7
Accounts payable	560	27.9	435	22.2	315	19.0
Accruals	150	7.5	130	6.6	90	5.4
Long-term debt	90	4.5	90	4.6	90	5.4
Total liabilities	1,030	51.3	945	48.2	805	48.5
Stock and surplus	210	10.4	210	10.7	210	12.7
Retained earnings	770	38.3	805	41.1	645	38.8
Total equity	980	48.7	1,015	51.8	855	51.5
Sales	5,100	100.0	4,270	100.0	3,260	100.0
Cost of sales	4,000	78.4	3,350	78.5	2,580	79.1
Operating exp.	900	17.7	810	19.0	770	23.6
Operating profit	200	3.9	110	2.5	(90)	(2.8)
Interest exp.	40	.8	65	1.5	70	2.1
Profit after tax	110	2.2	35	.8	(160)	(4.9)

and financing. A closer examination of the funds thrown off by the contracting assets would give a needed dynamic flair to the balance sheet.

A statement of changes in financial position restructured by Coleman[1] forms the basis for an analysis of cash flow for the ABC Company (see general cash flow analysis format at the end of this article).

Cash flow is not only provided by profits plus noncash charges, as the often used rule would have us believe. For example, when a company collects more than it bills to customers, receivables decrease, representing a positive flow of cash. When a company pays out more than is incurred in costs, payables decrease, representing a negative flow of cash. In general, an increase in assets or a decrease in liabilities or equity is a use of cash, while a decrease in assets or an increase in liabilities or equity from one balance statement to the next is a source of cash.

---

[1] Almand R. Coleman, "Restructuring the Statement of Changes in Financial Position," *Financial Executive*, Jan. 1979, p. 39.

Cash flow analysis for ABC

The cash flow analysis is divided into three important parts:

- cash for operations or internally generated cash,
- discretionary cash flows, and
- financing

Internally generated cash can only be estimated, and such a forecast depends on demand, net profit margin, and the ratio of volume-sensitive assets to volume-sensitive liabilities. Discretionary flows are mainly a product of management decision. Although closely related to sales volume, fixed assets of some companies may not increase in proportion to sales until management deems additional capacity necessary. The levels of long-term investments, other noncurrent assets, and dividends depend on the decision of management, and the levels of these items would not change in proportion to sales, especially in a period of steep decline in demand. The financing section summarizes the amount of debt necessary to finance operations and capital expenditures plus dividends, or it summarizes the amount of debt retired through excess funds from operations and from positive discretionary flows. The net change of the three major parts represents the total change in cash and equivalents on the balance sheet.

The cash flow analysis for the ABC Company (Figure 2) illustrates the difference between looking at a company's profits and looking at the cash flow. The operating flows and discretionary flows tend to have more effect on a company's debt service ability than do profits and depreciation. In 1980, even though profits and depreciation provided $70,000, an increasing inventory level which was counter to the general asset decrease, plus a disproportionately large decrease in accounts payable, resulted in an internal cash need of $55,000. The somewhat extroardinary need for cash for inventories and payables is further illustrated by the fact that inventories as a percent of assets increased from 58.2% to 63.2% in 1980, and payables decreased from 27.9% to 22.2%, as noted in Figure 1. Consequently, in 1980, $60,000 in additional debt plus $5,000 cash was necessary to finance operations and the $10,000 in capital expenditures.

In contrast, the negative "cash flow" of $140,000 in 1981, was exactly covered by operating flows since an orderly decrease in assets provided cash in excess of the amount required by declining liabilities. Thus, in 1981, in spite of a large net loss, only $20,000 in additional financing was required, and even this was to cover increased fixed assets.

Figure 2—Cash Flow Analysis—ABC Furniture Company ($000)
(Parentheses indicate a use of cash)

	1979	1980	1981
Sales	5,100	4,220	3,260
Assets	2,010	1,960	1,660
Profit plus noncash charges			
Net earnings (loss)		35	(160)
Depreciation/amortization		35	20
Total "cash flow"		70	(140)
Operating flows			
(Increase)/decrease in receivables		90	110
(Increase)/decrease in inventories		(70)	190
Increase/(decrease) in accts/payable		(125)	(120)
Increase/(decrease) in accruals		(20)	(40)
Total operating flows		(125)	140
I. Total cash generated internally		(55)	0
Discretionary flows			
(Acquired)/disposed of fixed assets		(10)	(20)
(Dividends paid)		—	—
II. Total discretionary flows		(10)	(20)
Financing			
Changes in stock and surplus		—	—
Increase/(decrease) in notes payable		60	20
Net increase/(decrease) in LTD		—	—
III. Total financing		60	20
IV. Net change in cash and equivalents from operations, discretionary flows, and financing		(5)	0

XYZ Lumber and Supply Company

The XYZ Company caters to building contractors, hoping to attract volume sales with a low mark-up. A substantial amount of financial leverage is used to gain a high return on investment. Aside from the untimely low-price/high-volume strategy, the company's second mistake was to gear up for a housing recovery in 1981 in their area, which never occurred.

The financial statement spread for XYZ Company (Figure 3) shows that levels of most major assets and liabilities, except for accounts payable, remained steady as a percent of assets from 1979 to 1980. Profits declined mostly as a result of decreased sales, as the operating margin indicates only a slight decrease in operating efficiency between 1979 and 1980.

Figure 3—XYZ Lumber and Supply Company (Dollars in thousands)

	1979	%	1980	%	1981	%
Cash	60	1.3	20	.5	10	.2
Accounts receiv.	2,500	55.1	2,060	55.4	2,210	49.6
Inventory	1,440	31.7	1,200	32.3	1,670	37.4
Fixed assets	420	9.3	410	11.0	540	12.1
Other assets	120	2.6	30	.8	30	.7
Total assets	4,540	100.0	3,720	100.0	4,460	100.0
Notes payable	1,350	29.7	1,110	29.8	1,530	34.3
Current mat.—LTD	300	6.6	130	3.5	50	1.1
Accounts payable	1,100	24.2	850	22.9	1,280	28.7
Accruals	530	11.7	330	8.9	370	8.3
Long-term debt	240	5.3	100	2.7	150	3.4
Total liabilities	3,520	77.5	2,520	67.8	3,380	75.8
Stock and surplus	250	5.5	280	7.5	280	6.3
Retained earnings	770	17.0	920	24.7	800	17.9
Total equity	1,020	22.5	1,200	32.2	1,080	24.2
Sales	17,700	100.0	16,100	100.0	13,400	100.0
Cost of sales	15,300	86.4	13,900	86.3	11,600	86.6
Operating exp.	1,800	10.2	1,750	10.9	1,700	12.7
Operating profit	600	3.4	450	2.8	100	.7
Interest exp.	300	1.7	230	1.4	225	1.7
Profit after tax	220	1.2	150	.9	(120)	(.9)

In 1981, inventories and fixed assets were increased in anticipation of an upturn in business. These increases were supported by increases in debt and accounts payable. The operating profit margin of .7% of sales in 1981 is a direct result of a definite hike in the level of operating expenses that year. Even though interest expenses are declining in absolute terms, the increased level of interest as a percent of sales ultimately left the company with a net loss after taxes.

Cash flow analysis for XYZ

The cash flow analysis for XYZ Company (Figure 4) shows the orderly decrease in sales-related assets and liabilities in 1980, as summarized by the amount of total cash generated internally. Asset decreases in excess of liability decreases contributed more to this figure than did profits and depreciation. Internal cash and a small amount of discretionary flows were used to reduce short- and long-term debt (including current maturities). The analysis in 1981 illustrates how the net loss coupled with the anticipatory expansion of assets

Figure 4—Cash Flow Analysis—XYZ Lumber and Supply Company ($000) (Parentheses indicate a use of cash)

	1979	1980	1981
Sales	17,700	16,100	13,400
Assets	4,540	3,720	4,460
Profit plus noncash charges			
Net earnings (loss)		150	(120)
Depreciation/amortization		25	30
Total "cash flow"		175	(90)
Operating flows			
(Increase)/decrease in receivables		440	(150)
(Increase)/decrease in inventories		240	(470)
Increase/(decrease) in accts/payable		(250)	430
Increase/(decrease) in accruals		(200)	40
Total operating flows		230	(150)
I. Total cash generated internally		405	(240)
Discretionary flows			
(Acquired)/disposed of fixed assets		(15)	(160)
(Increase)/decrease in other assets		90	—
(Dividends paid)		—	—
II. Total discretionary flows		75	(160)
Financing			
Changes in stock and surplus		30	—
Increase/(decrease) in notes payable		(240)	420
Increase/(decrease) in LTD		(310)	(30)
III. Total financing		(520)	390
IV. Net change in cash and equivalents from operations, discretionary flows, and financing		(40)	(10)

caused a large needs for cash, both internally and for discretionary flows, necessitating a considerable amount of additional financing.

Ratio analysis of the two companies

Selected ratios of the two companies (Figure 5) give evidence of some important points in analyzing a recession-sensitive firm:

1. The ratio of debt/net worth may not increase substantially during periods of depressed sales and profits if a firm is not highly leveraged. However, a

Figure 5—Ratio Analysis

	1979	1980	1981
ABC Furniture Company			
Sales ($000)	5,100	4,270	3,260
Assets ($000)	2,010	1,960	1,660
Sales/assets	2.5	2.2	2.0
Debt/net worth	1.1	.9	.9
Receivables turnover (days)	40	40	41
Inventory turnover (days)	106	135	149
Payables turnover (days)	51	47	45
Net profit margin	2.2%	.8%	(4.9%)
XYZ Lumber and Supply Company			
Sales ($000)	17,700	16,100	13,400
Assets ($000)	4,540	3,720	4,460
Sales/assets	3.9	4.3	3.0
Debt/net worth	3.5	2.1	3.1
Receivables turnover (days)	52	46	60
Inventory turnover (days)	34	32	52
Payables turnover (days)	26	22	40
Net profit margin	1.2%	.9%	(.9%)

leveraged firm such as the XYZ Company will show an increasing debt/net worth because comparable losses extract a greater percentage of a lower level of equity.

2. A recessionary period makes various "financial sins" more prominent than during an expansionary period. The amount of obsolete and slow moving inventory in the ABC Company is now more apparent, as is the burden of the recent inventory buildup of the XYZ Company.

Financial inefficiencies in the income statement are often hidden or ignored in an expanding era, when the expenses on a percentage of sales basis do not seem troublesome. In a recessionary era, tumbling sales tend to make certain expenses in absolute dollars appear unjustified with the reduced level of output. Even discounting such emerging extravagances, when the economy cools off, sales contract faster than costs and expenses, putting a general strain on gross margins and operating margins.

3. The periods of turnover of receivables and payables give an indication of the characteristics and attitudes of customers and creditors and the extent to which *they* are affected by the economic slump. ABC Company presents an example of steady receivables turnover and decreasing payables turnover. One might theorize that ABC Company is holding its own credit policies firm in order to preserve cash flow and that they are paying more promptly in response

to pressure from creditors. For XYZ Company, on the other hand, an apparently relaxing credit stand both to customers and from creditors has allowed turnover periods of receivables and payables to increase.

Future operations

Now that trends in financial structure, profitability, and the company reactions during the recession have been noted, the loan officer is naturally interested in what the future holds for the customer's operations. Can the company endure a sales slump for another year, or will losses be compounded to a terminal extent, no matter how efficiently the flow of cash is regulated? If the economy improves, is the firm in a good position for recovery, or will well-positioned competition be the beneficiaries of increasing demand?

Forecasts must deal with uncertainties of demand, operating efficiencies, interest rates, and the amount of cash provided or required by the changes in operating levels.

Forecasting internal generation of cash

Changes in demand and the ability of the firm to maintain profitable operations in a recessionary period may require many changing assumptions. As in any forecast, your customer's conclusions are only as good as the logical nature of the forecast's assumptions. Every assumption explains the creation of a need or a source of new funds. A tool to forecast financial and cash position, more flexible than generating pro forma statements and allowing quicker sensitivity analysis, is necessary for a credit proposal with many inherent uncertainties.

Figure 6—MFG Company

Sales—$5,000,000 Net Profit—3% of Sales Depreciation—1% of Sales
Projected Sales—$5,750,000

Assets		% of Sales	Liabilities		% of Sales
Cash	$ 50,000	N/A	Payables	$ 375,000	7.5
Receivables	675,000	13.5	Accruals	250,000	5.0
Inventories	750,000	15.0	Notes payable	125,000	N/A
Fixed assets	1,025,000	N/A	LTD	625,000	N/A
Total assets	$2,500,000		Equity	1,125,000	N/A
		28.5			12.5

The elements of a pro forma statement are either related to sales volume, regulated by management decision, or are the plug figures for debt and cash, which tell how much money is needed or left over. The cash flow analysis used earlier contains these same elements and most, if not all, assumptions deal with the figure of internally generated cash, which is that part dependent on sales volume and operating efficiency. Therefore, the prediction of cash internally generated will automatically tell of a cash need or a cash surplus after consideration of discretionary flows.

MFG Manufacturing Company

Consider the MFG Company, a manufacturing firm (see Figure 6). Assets which are assumed to be related to volume are expressed as a percent of sales of the base year. With other factors held constant, for every additional $1.00 in sales, 28.5¢ will be required for additional assets, and 12.5¢ will be provided by additional liabilities. The remaining 16¢ will have to be financed from additional debt or equity and from additional profits to retained earnings. A formula for predicting the need for external funds[2] contains essentials for forecasting internal cash generation, after some adjustments.

$$\text{Internal Cash Generated} = (M + D)S^* + \frac{L}{S}(S^* - S) - \frac{A}{S}(S^* - S) \text{ where:}$$

M = Net profit as a percent of sales.

D = Depreciation as a percent of sales.

$\frac{L}{S}$ = Liabilities that increase or decrease proportionately with sales, as a percent of sales.

$\frac{A}{S}$ = Assets that increase or decrease proportionately with sales, as a percent of sales.

S = Present yearly sales figure.

S^* = Projected yearly sales figure.

For the MFG Company (dollars in thousands):

$$\begin{aligned}\text{Internal cash generated} &= (.03 + .01)\ 5{,}750 + (.125)\ (750) - (.285)\ (750) \\ &= (.04)\ 5{,}750 - (.16)\ (750) \\ &= 230 - 120 \\ &= 110\end{aligned}$$

Profits plus depreciation and increasing liabilities are sources of cash, while increasing assets are uses of cash, during a period of profitability and expansion. The profitability and financial structure of MFG Company would generate

---

[2] J. Fred Weston and Eugene F. Brigham. *Managerial Finance,* 1978, p. 96–97.

$76,250 internally over the next year with the given increase in sales. If this will not cover planned dividends and capital expenditures, the company will need to seek external financing through additional debt or equity; cash reserves will also be affected.

. . . now back to the recession. MFG forecasts a 15% decrease in sales, with all other factors remaining the same. A sales decrease will require some alteration of the formula regarding the sources and uses of cash: Declining assets are now a source of cash along with profit and depreciation, and declining liabilities become a use of cash.

$$\begin{aligned}\text{Internal cash generated} &= (.03 + .01)\,4{,}250 - (.125)\,(750) + (.285)\,(750)\\ &= (.04)\,4{,}250 + (.16)\,(750)\\ &= 170 + 120\\ &= 290\end{aligned}$$

Thus, $290,000 will be provided for dividends and capital expenditures, but much of the internally generated cash must be used to reduce debt to keep a consistent financial structure. If assets are decreasing and are supported in part by bank financing, then bank financing should also be reduced by excess cash flows.

Sensitivity analysis

The MFG Company later admits that due to costs decreasing more slowly than sales, higher interest rates, and a few possible write-offs, the net profit margin could possibly drop as low as a 3% loss on sales. Therefore,

$$\begin{aligned}\text{Internal cash generated} &= (-.03 + .01)\,4{,}250 - (.125)\,(750) + (.285)\,(750)\\ &= (-.02)4{,}250 + (.16)\,(750)\\ &= -85 + 120\\ &= 35 \text{ or } \$35{,}000\end{aligned}$$

With the net loss becoming a use of funds in addition to the declining liabilities, the declining assets do not provide much in excess internal cash. One might question the logic of any dividends or capital expenditures, in light of the amount that debt must be reduced to salvage a respectable capital structure. Heavier losses could eventually create a negative flow of internal cash, and the financial structure would be in strong need of additional owner investment.

The extent to which $(\frac{L}{S} - \frac{A}{S})\,(S^* - S)$ is a use of cash in an expanding period and a source of cash in a period of contraction is the difference between the percentages of sales-related assets and sales-related liabilities. With a difference of .16, as in the previous examples, $120,000 was the amount of cash provided or needed, depending on whether sales and assets were decreasing or increasing.

When assets are supported to a greater extent by payables and accruals, such as a total of 15% rather than 12.5%, then $(\frac{L}{S} - \frac{A}{S})$ becomes .135 rather than .16, and 750,000 (.135) = $101,250 which would be provided in a contracting era or needed in an expanding era. This simply means that the more external funds support sales-sensitive assets, the more external funds will be needed or reduced when these assets increase or decrease.

The internal cash generation formula can be used quickly to conduct sensitivity analyses, as has been done with the changing profit margin of the MFG Company. A company's future cash flows can also be readily estimated under different rates of change in demand and with different percentages of sales-supportive assets and liabilities. The formula, as presented, can be directly related to the cash flow analysis format. However, alterations in the formula can be made, such as taking depreciation as a percentage out and adding in a dollar amount to the final figure, if depreciation does not historically relate well to sales. Fixed assets or other noncurrent assets could be inserted into the equation as a separate term, $\frac{FA}{S}(S^* - S)$, if it is found that these items are closely related to demand and account for a consistent source or use of cash, with a given change in sales.

The internal cash formula, affordable growth rate formulas, and any others relying on ratios of sales to assets are limited because levels of assets and turnover periods are seldom constant. However, the absolute effect of a tightened credit policy, inventory buildup, etc. could be estimated and considered in the final figure of cash generated, and the advantages of simplicity and speed over pro forma statements would be maintained. In the case of companies such as the ABC and XYZ companies, the formula would give an indication of the consequences to cash flow when items which should change with sales, ultimately do not.

The loan officer as financial consultant

As the loan officer becomes more enlightened about a company's future, given all of the uncertainties involved, he or she is in a position to give financial guidance. The manager of a company troubled by a continuing recession may not approach recession management with the same degree of forethought and strategic planning which accompanies successful operations during an era of increasing demand. The business manager often equates success with output

Figure 7—Cash Flow Analysis—Sample Company (Parentheses indicate a use of cash)

	1979	1980	1981
Sales	____	____	____
Assets	____	____	____
Profits plus noncash charges			
Net earnings (loss)		____	____
Depreciation/amortization		____	____
Deferred taxes		____	____
Total "cash flow"		____	____
Operating flows			
(Increase)/decrease in receivables		____	____
(Increase)/decrease in inventories		____	____
(Increase)/decrease in other curr. assets		____	____
Increase/(decrease) in accts. payable		____	____
Increase/(decrease) in accruals		____	____
Increase/(decrease) in taxes payable		____	____
Increase/(decrease) in other curr. liab.		____	____
Total operating flows		____	____
I. Total cash generated internally		====	====
Discretionary flows			
(Acquired)/disposed of fixed assets		____	____
(Increase)/decrease in investments		____	____
(Increase)/decrease in other assets		____	____
(Dividends paid)		____	____
II. Total discretionary cash flow		====	====
Financing			
Changes in stock and surplus		____	____
Increase/(decrease) in notes/payable		____	____
Increase/(decrease) in LTD		____	____
III. Total financing		====	====
IV. Net change in cash and equivalents from operations, discretionary flows, and financing		====	====

and earnings and may want to optimistically position a firm for a time in the future when conditions are quantitatively better.

In such cases, the outside objectivity of the loan officer as a financial consultant—working with a general cash flow analysis format such as in Figure 7—can help managers understand that management of a recession is vital to a firm. As a manager presents forecasts of increasing sales and profits, the loan officer can temper an over-positive outlook with a variety of other estimates of demand and profitability, some of which may more closely approach reality. A quick prediction of future cash flows under varying conditions, using the internal cash formula and allowing criticism or agreement by the customer, will lead to an easier understanding of future financial restructuring and debt repayment capabilities of the firm.

Once the manager can admit the possibility of a continued recessionary period, a contingency plan should be developed. A company which has had problems and is convinced that a solution has been found, should be able to give a detailed, specific plan for what it intends to do. Contingency plans for orderly and systematic cutbacks, as well as sales stimulation, should be set in motion as soon as a decline in orders is realized, rather than later after the real output has fallen. With companies which are particularly sensitive to a recession, the loan officer can encourage efforts to trim overhead and operations to maintain profitability. These companies are now prepared to lead their way through a recession, rather than apprehensively to react or struggle under externally imposed conditions over which they have little control.

Summary

A rapidly expanding company may not be able to sustain rapid growth and still keep a sound financial structure. A recession-sensitive company normally has cash flow from decreasing assets but may still have trouble enduring the low-demand periods, especially if net losses become common. With the aid of the internal cash generation formula, the loan officer will better understand changes on the balance sheet and in operations and can foresee potential cash flow problems. Such tools and concepts allow a loan officer to judge how well a company is managed during periods when the level of assets and operations is subject to large decreases or increases.

Making reasonable judgments about future changes in financial structure and ability to repay obligations to the bank under various possible conditions will be a relatively quick project. With a large number of possible scenarios flashing before their eyes, lenders can help a manager keep a step ahead of financial crisis. To encourage, or even stipulate by agreement, cutbacks and improvements which will promote profitability when faced with decreased demand or anticipated expansion will protect the interests of both lender and borrower. □

Bibliography

Coleman, Almand R., "Restructuring the Statement of Changes in Financial Positions." *Financial Executive,* January 1979, p. 39.

Weston, J. Fred and Eugene F. Brigham. Managerial Finance. Hinsdale, Illinois: The Dryden Press, 1978, pp. 96–97.

Financial Statement Analysis

Examining Personal Financial Statements

by Christopher Volk

There are two distinctly different means of personal financial statement analysis. The most commonly observed method is that of net worth examination, which essentially is designed to estimate the liquidity of the individual in the event asset liquidation must be relied on to repay obligations. The second and more complex method is that of cash flow estimation which relies on the preparation of an individual statement of changes in financial position.

The author is in real estate acquisitions, Franchise Finance Corporation of America, Phoenix, Arizona. At the time this article was published in May 1984, he was a corporate loan officer, National Bank of Georgia, Atlanta, Georgia.

Generally, personal asset, or net worth, liquidation is a secondary source of repayment for borrowings. The primary source of repayment is normally estimated personal future income or the projected future cash flow of a closely-held corporation. As a result, personal financial statements often must be examined in order to estimate the amount of independent support offered to a proposed credit extension by the secondary support of individual net worths and personal cash flows. In regard to independent support offered by a personal net worth, the analyst must estimate the amount of asset liquidation which could be reasonably expected to occur in order to satisfy bank indebtedness. If an individual cash flow is available which is fully independent from the primary source of repayment—that is, the primary repayment source is not a closely-held concern from which a sole source of income is derived—the cash flow of the individual may also be examined. Individual cash flow will be discussed in greater detail later.

Determining net worth support

Personal financial statements are often intended to present customers and loan guarantors in the best light possible. Accordingly, a reported personal income and asset values can often be overstated. For example, income is very frequently gross corporate revenues or "estimated future income," rather than historic personal earnings. Real estate is often valued exorbitantly above liquidation or even fair market values. And the same can often be said about accounts receivable, investments, personal effects, and most other asset categories. The analyst must be cognizant of such embellishments and consider instead the individual's net worth at a realizable liquidation value. In the same light, the analyst must consider in whose name the assets are titled. Individuals frequently report net worths which are composed primarily of assets held jointly with their spouses or others. Similarly, income is frequently the combined earnings of both the individual and the spouse. Only the assets of the guarantor should be displayed. If no assets are held individually, then a joint guarantee with a spouse may be more desirable.

Liquidity of assets

Personal financial statements should be spread with assets listed in order of their liquidity. Generally speaking, personal effects such as household furnishings, automobiles, and the like should be omitted, since their highly illiquid nature likens them more to living expenditures than assets with realizable liquidation values. In this respect, it is often necessary for the analyst to use personal judgment in deciding which, if any, assets should be eliminated from the spread. Classic cars, art, antique furniture, and jewelry collections may merit inclusion in your spread.

The analyst should also consider eliminating any reported assets which relate to the primary source of debt repayment. For example, if the individual is a guarantor of the indebtedness of a closely-held corporation, the value of the corporation should be eliminated. Presumably, if the corporation cannot repay its own obligations, then its value is questionable anyway. Similarly, if the individual not only guarantees the debt but has granted the bank a second lien on wholly-owned real estate, that real estate should also be eliminated in order to arrive at an estimate of fully independent net worth support. Obviously, if an individual's net worth is centered primarily in wholly-owned real estate already pledged to the bank on the same indebtedness, then his remaining net worth likely adds nominal, if any, support to the loan.

Validating asset valuation

By far the greatest difficulty in determining net worth support is validating asset valuation. As will be later examined with preparing a cash flow, the analyst should discuss each item with the customer, knowing both the original cost of the asset and the method of market valuation employed by the individual. Reasonableness of market values may also be supported by available independent real estate or other appraisals.

In becoming satisfied with the reasonableness of market values, the analyst should note to what extent this represents a departure from the cost basis of the assets. Gains realized from asset liquidation entail the mandatory payment of capital gains tax. A reserve for capital gains tax should therefore be estimated by the analyst and shown as a liability.

In the event a Keogh or IRA plan is reported, a 10% penalty is assessed for early withdrawal, with the remainder taxed at the personal marginal rate. A reserve for such an early withdrawal penalty and income taxes should also be estimated by the analyst and shown as a liability. Vested corporate pension plans normally cannot be liquidated until retirement.

Contingent liabilities

Last, the analyst must consider the contingent liabilities of the individual. Is the individual the subject of any lawsuits? Is the individual a comaker, endorser, or guarantor on any other obligations? And is the individual contingently liable for any partnership obligations as a general partner? Often the apparent support of individual net worths to bank borrowings can be severely diminished by such contingent liabilities since the bank may ultimately find itself grouped with other creditors with each having equal claims against the individual.

Ultimately, the capacity of an individual's net worth to offer liquidation support to bank indebtedness is wholly dependent on the character and personal integrity of the borrower. To this end, a "comfort level" can be attained through historic transaction experience, personal experience, credit bureau reports, and an examination of personal asset composition. A preponderance of personal luxury items may indicate a "flashy" lifestyle while a nominal net worth compared to income indicates an evident inability to save. Conversely frugality is often exhibited by relatively liquid net worths, little indebtedness, and little asset replacement or improvement. While the integrity of the individual should result in fairly stated financial data, the personal statement should always be prepared on the bank's own form. In this manner, the financial information is officially addressed to the bank which will have legal recourse in the event that extensive misleading embellishments or asset transfers occur.

Guide to spreading personal financial statements in order to estimate cash flow

Unlike corporate financial statements, personal statements are seldom prepared which employ consistent accounting and asset valuation principles. Nor are personal financial statements consistently prepared at the individual's fiscal year-end (December 31). As a result, spreading personal financial statements to estimate cash flow can be a tedious task which demands numerous explanations of accounts by the customer. For example, real estate is frequently assigned increasingly higher values from year to year. While this may be indicative of true value and, hence, net worth, it can hardly be indicative of actual cash flow (which repays bank indebtedness). Thus, an increase in real estate values may not mean that new property was acquired or even that cash improvements were made to existing property, but rather that unrealized appreciation has been recognized. This is a violation of generally accepted accounting principles (GAAP) employed in corporate financial statements. These principles prohibit the recognition of gains on the sale of assets until title to the property has been exchanged.

Questioning the customer

The majority of bank customers are unaware of GAAP and, as previously mentioned, their personal financial statements are often intended to show them only in the best light possible. As a result, the analyst must make alterations in spreading a personal financial statement in order to help determine cash flow. Preferably, all assets should be restated at cost. Where this is not possible, one year may be used as a base year with assets maintaining constant values in subsequent years. This will often involve detailed questioning of the customer.

For example, one might ask the customer if the increased real estate value was at all representative of cash purchases or property improvements. Here are other questions that might be asked: Was the increased value of closely-held corporate stock indicative of an actual equity infusion or merely revaluation? Was the increase or decrease in the reported value of an art collection actually indicative of acquisitions or divestitures? And was cash actually paid for the part ownership of a syndicated limited partnership? Each balance sheet item should be examined to see if cash was actually expended in the acquisition of that item. If assets were acquired without cash, they should be omitted. New assets should always be listed on their cost basis with the remaining assets carrying their values from the base year.

In this manner, one may determine the extent of net worth increases on a cost or cash basis. Note that estimating cash flow entails distinct departures from the examination of net worth support already discussed. Disregard, for example, the estimation of any capital gains tax liability, since such an estimate implies the forthcoming liquidation of assets which would result in such a liability. Instead, the aim here is to examine the individual as a "going concern."

In addition, personal effects should most likely be included in the spread when examining cash flow unless they are insignificant items such as clothing or other transient personal effects. Frequently, net worth increases on a cash basis may relate largely to the acquisition of a car, boat, furnishings, or other personal effects. Unless these items are included in the spread, the extent of any net worth increase on a cash basis may be understated.

The increase or decrease in net worth from period to period is called the net worth variance. Naturally, a cost basis increase in net worth must always be less than the customer's available cash flow for the period since some cash flow will be expended on personal living costs. In effect, a positive net worth variance indicates that a portion of earnings has been retained.

Personal spread

Much can be determined from the preparation of a personal spread. The lack of a positive net worth variance on a cost basis indicates the maintenance of a lifestyle which requires virtually all the available cash flow. On the other hand, the presence of a positive net worth variance is an indicator of discretionary available cash flow for new debt service. Figure 1 gives a suggested format for spreading personal financial statements in order to determine cash flow.

Estimating cash flow

At this point, it should be a simple matter to see that a personal net worth variance can be likened to corporate net income. In other words, a positive net worth variance is what is left over from all sources of income after living expenses have been subtracted. On the other hand, a negative net worth variance indicates that living expenditures have outstripped income; a personal loss has occurred which has been funded by asset liquidation or borrowing. Determining the cause for the net worth variance can be instrumental in estimating the adequacy of cash flows for debt service requirements.

Figure 2 provides a suggested guide for spreading personal cash flow which closely resembles a corporate cash flow model. Generally speaking, personal cash generated by operations will be equal to the net worth variance. This is a natural result of the fact that personal net income is normally recorded on a

Figure 1—Suggested Personal Financial Statement Spread

Assets	Liabilities and net worth
Cash	Notes payable to banks—unsecured
Stocks and securities—listed	Notes payable to banks—secured
Cash value life insurance	Real estate mortgages payable
Notes and accounts receivable	Notes payable to others
Stocks and securities—other	Accounts payable
Real estate—wholly owned	Total liabilities
Real estate—undivided interest	Beginning net worth
Investments in limited partnerships	Net worth variance
Other assets	Ending net worth
Total assets	Total liabilities and net worth
	Current debt maturities
	Contingent liabilities

cash basis and does not have to be converted from an accrual basis of accounting. In calculating a personal cash flow then, one simply reconciles the net worth variance to changes in balance sheet items from period to period. While this exercise may provide an informative explanation of sources and uses of cash for the period reviewed, it eliminates any examination of the income statement. Rather, the only data presently used are that of net income or the net worth variance. Since individuals do not prepare income statements in the corporate sense, it will be necessary to fill in the available income information while estimating the remainder of the income statement.

Sources of income

Salary is by and large the single most prevalent source of discretionary cash flow. Other frequent sources of income include gains on the sale of assets, rents, interest, and dividends, among others. The most reliable source of income information is a personal federal income tax return. Special care should be exercised when extracting income data to recognize the extent of noncash transactions or deductions which serve as popular tax shelters. Depreciation passed through limited partnership interests, business interests, or rental property is the most common such noncash deduction although there are others. Therefore, "adjusted gross income" as it appears on a tax return may hardly be representative of the actual cash income figure which should appear on the personal cash flow statement.

If a federal income tax return is unavailable, it will be necessary to pose detailed questions to the individual in order to examine the income statement. First, the full extent of cash salary must be known in addition to cash income

Figure 2—Suggested Guide for Spreading Personal Cash Flow

Income Statement:
  Cash salary
  Other recurring cash revenues
  Nonrecurring income
  Gain/loss on asset sales
  Less: Living expense*
    Nonrecurring expenses

Discretionary cash flow (net worth variance)
  Adjustments to income
  Decrease (increase) accounts receivable
  Increase (decrease) accounts payable and accruals
  Cash generated by operations

  Less:
  Increased assets
  Reduced liabilities
  Total nonoperating sources:
  Add:
  Increased liabilities
  Reduced assets
  Total nonoperating uses
  Net nonoperating sources (uses)
  Increase (decrease) cash

* Includes interest, income taxes, and all other living expenditures. Increased detail may be used if desired.

---

derived from interest, rents, and dividends and other recurring income sources. Second, the actual sales price of any assets liquidated must be known. For example, if real estate is sold, the analyst must inquire as to the actual sales price, which will likely be higher than the base value it was carried at in prior years. The difference between the sales price and the base value is the gain on the asset sale which appears in the income statement. The actual base value of the asset liquidated will have already been calculated in the initial phase of preparing the cash flow analysis. Last, the extent of any nonrecurring income outside of asset sales must be known.

Once all the cash income has been documented, the difference between cash income and the net worth variance must equal estimated living expenditures. If a personal federal income tax return is available, greater detail may be added to this category to reduce the plug figure to as minimal an amount as feasible; taxes, health expenditures, interest payments, and various other cash expenditures can be easily extracted from the customer's itemized deductions list. Any nonrecurring expenditures should also be recorded.

Estimating future recurring cash income and living expenditures

On completing the personal cash flow statement, valuable insight can be gained through the estimation of future recurring cash income and living expenditures in regard to the ability of the individual to meet future debt maturities. Needless to say, the greater the detail in the income statement, the better the understanding of the ability of the individual to repay bank borrowings. Personal financial statement spreading occasionally requires that common sense estimates be made due to the aforementioned inconsistency and inaccuracy which frequently characterizes personal financial data.

For example, does reported compensation and income appear reasonable in light of both the sources and reported net worth? Were all assets consistently listed from year to year, or were some unwittingly omitted in one or more periods? And are the reported cash revenues for a period of time equivalent to the period elapsed since the last financial statement received? If the net worth variance is for a 15-month period, the customer's cash revenues must be estimated for the same period. Answers not readily available to these and other questions may entail the preparation of estimates which appear more reasonable to the analyst.

Conclusion

Two methods of spreading personal financial statements have been examined. The first is a means of determining the estimated fair market value of net worth to ascertain secondary repayment support. The second is a means of determining individual net income and estimated recurring cash flow as a means to determine primary or secondary repayment source adequacy. The former considers the individual as a liquidating concern. The latter considers the individual as a going concern, very much akin to the way a corporation is considered in accordance with GAAP. In this case, the capacity of the individual to continue to generate cash from operations is the considered source of bank debt repayment. The secondary source may be the liquidation of a specific asset held as collateral, a personal guarantee, or some other security.

In general, too, an individual with personal indebtedness is, in effect, a guarantor on his own debt for which the liquidation value of his net worth may add some measure of support. Personal financial statement analysis is, in many ways, more complex than the analysis of corporate financial statements. Individual financial data are prepared frequently at inconsistent dates in an inconsistent manner using unknown principles of accounting and asset valuation. As a result, spreading personal financial data for determining net worth support and cash flow requires that numerous questions be asked of the individual before any true comprehension can be gained. Given thorough analysis, personal financial data can be spread and analyzed effectively to foretell net worth support and debt service ability. □

Using Tax Returns as Credit Analysis Tools

by Maurice F. Claeys

Credit analysis is the continual testing for the logic in the borrower's repayment plan. Inconsistencies that upset the logic are clues to the need for further analysis. Making tax returns a part of the credit decision and loan management process can give loan officers an advantage in accomplishing the task.

The author is senior vice president, Rainier National Bank, Seattle, Washington, and currently on leave as consultant to the Agency for International Development, U.S. Department of State.

Income tax returns can be effective credit analysis tools, whether you are making a loan to an individual, sole proprietorship, corporation, or partnership. The tale of promise and hope the prospective borrower weaves for you in applying for the loan is frequently the antithesis of the story of woe and misfortune the borrower tells the tax collector. By itself, such a discrepancy may not prompt you to turn down the loan request. But it should prompt you to begin asking questions of the borrower to get a good explanation of why the numbers don't match up. If the customer can't explain the differences in the numbers to your satisfaction, you probably should not make the loan.

At Rainier Bank, we make it a practice to require at least three years' tax returns as part of the commercial loan credit analysis process in dealing with small corporations and partnerships and in evaluating commercial loan requests from individuals. In dealing with such customers, tax returns are required of those seeking credit and of those personally guaranteeing credit. We do not look on tax records as a replacement for financial statements but rather as a support for them. Tax returns provide us with additional risk evaluation information.

The tax return can serve a number of purposes:

• It can help verify income. This is essential if you are making a loan to a self-employed individual.

• It can give you a more complete picture of the borrower's interest expenses than you might find on the financial statement.

• It can give you an idea of the sorts of tax shelters the borrower may be using. If the IRS doesn't like any of them, your customer could be facing increased tax liability. If that results in a reduction in the customer's cash flow, it could endanger your loan repayment.

• It can provide business development opportunities.

Whenever a significant difference exists between the numbers reported on the tax return and the assets and liabilities listed on the finanical statement, we like to have the customer submit an IRS Schedule M1, which itemizes these differences. This is an easy and convenient way for the customer to explain the variances and for the lending officer to obtain an understanding of why they exist.

Lending to individuals

Tax return's chief benefit

In loans to individuals, the tax return's chief benefit is the verification it provides of salary, commission, interest, and other income. Very few people overstate their income to Uncle Sam, but some people are not above exaggerating their income on a loan application. It is particularly useful in verifying the income of professional people—doctors, lawyers, and the like—or any other self-employed individual who is unable to produce standard income verification, such as a W-2 form.

In one instance at Rainier, a self-employed applicant provided a financial statement as part of his loan request that showed his total net income as $62,000. A review of his 1982 tax records, however, showed a total taxable income of $31,000. In 1983, he reported a loss on his tax returns and showed no taxable income. One of the problems we had with the financial statement supplied by the customer was that it did not indicate the time frame for which the asset and liability information was being reported. In the end, we were unable to get a satisfactory answer from the customer concerning why the income he was reporting to us was so much different from the income reported for tax purposes. We declined the loan request.

Other benefits

Beyond a verification of income, a close look at an individual's tax return can reveal liabilities or impediments to the customer's debt-servicing ability that were not revealed in discussions with the customer or on the loan application. Is the person taking a tax deduction for exceptionally high medical expenses? Does he or she have more dependents than you were led to believe? Are alimony payments revealed on the tax return higher than you believed them to be? Any circumstances such as these could reduce the customer's disposable income, leading to problems with loan repayment.

Lending to sole proprietorships

Objective benefits

In many small business loan transactions, especially sole proprietorships, the tax returns may be your only source of information about profit/loss and cash flow, because the business may be too small to justify the expense of obtaining a CPA-prepared financial statement. Again, you want to compare the tax return with the statement numbers, if available, to see if the two match. And if they don't, you shouldn't make the loan without a satisfactory explanation.

The differences could be explained in a number of ways. One reason might be that the bookkeeping approach the customer used to generate the financial statement numbers differs from the tax accounting approach, resulting in different figures. Maybe the financial statement numbers (if they were prepared after the tax information) are larger because the customer has had dramatically increased sales recently. On the other hand, maybe the customer has no satisfactory explanation. In any event, ask the questions. And if you don't like the answers, don't make the loan.

Subjective benefits

On a more subjective level, the tax returns of a small business can give you an insight into the borrower's business acumen and management ability. Look over the capital gains and losses the borrower reports. A history of wise and profitable investments indicates that the borrower knows how to use money to make money. However, a history of investment losses should not automatically make you skeptical about the borrower's ability to manage properly the money he wants to borrow from you. How depreciation and amortization are calculated for tax purposes can show a loss for the business without demonstrating poor financial management.

For example, if your customer has real estate investments, he or she will want to take advantage of taxable losses, especially in the early years of the investments. It could be that the tax records you are looking at are for the years in which the investor elected to take such a loss. The investment itself could, in the long run, prove profitable. Reviewing the customer's investment record can also allow you to verify dividend income.

Lending to corporations and partnerships

It is Rainier Bank's practice to seek a professionally prepared financial statement from corporations and partnerships, but we still like to have the tax information. We use the tax reports to verify the financial statement numbers and analyze the company's ability to secure and repay the loan. Here are some of the things we like to see our loan officers do:

- Compare the tax liability stated on the financial statement with the tax liability listed on the tax return. If they differ, find out why.

• Differences in the way in which sales and expenses are recognized may also account for the differences in the tax liability figures. Frequently, it's because of deferred taxes. For example, the Internal Revenue Service allows accelerated depreciation of five years and 22% in the first year, 37% in the second. Generally accepted accounting principles require that the asset be depreciated over its entire useful life.

• Look at the capital gains and losses to see how the company has recently disposed of assets. The frequent selling of the type of assets the customer wants to use to secure the loan should make the lender wary of the loan transaction. Will the security be there if we need to turn to it to service the debt?

• Ask the customer to explain any balance sheet changes between year-ends and compare the balance sheet numbers with those on the financial statement.

• Review the tax returns for an idea of the company's capital expenditures. Do they match corresponding expenditures in the loan application?

• If it's an agricultural loan, use tax Schedule F to document the cash flow stated on the agricultural budget.

• Use the tax return to verify company ownership and officers' salaries.

Business development

Tax returns can enhance business development beyond the making of the loan:

• You can suggest that an individual retirement account (IRA) or Keogh be opened if the customer does not work under a pension plan or if he or she has a high tax liability and could benefit from a shelter.

• Corporations without an existing pension plan might be directed to your Trust Department which can assist the company in setting one up.

• Review the customer's interest income. You might be able to show him or her the advantages of opening or expanding deposit services with your bank.

• Individuals with sufficient income might benefit from private banking services.

Drawbacks

Income tax returns as a credit analysis tool are not without their drawbacks which should be borne in mind. To begin with, they are prepared annually, so the information may not be timely. However, by reviewing the last two to three years' returns, you can get an idea of any financial patterns exhibited by the customer and obtain a feel for the customer's overall business success.

Depending on the nature of the company's business, special industry tax incentives may make the tax return asset/liability picture appear bleaker than it really is. You have to do a little investigating. Perhaps you'll find that the would-be borrower is in better financial shape than the return would indicate.

As with just about everything in life, timing plays an important role in the preparation of tax returns. Through proper planning, the customer can manipulate the timing of certain transactions, such as accounts, receivable billings, the incurring of prepaid expenses, and asset purchases, to obtain a more favorable tax position. In the process, the tax return numbers may prove unreliable in the credit analysis process. Question the customer to find out what part the timing element played in the tax return preparation.

Conclusion

The success or failure of credit analysis rests on the ability of the loan officer to make an intelligent, well-informed credit decision and to manage the risk properly once the loan is on the books. Making tax returns a part of the credit decision and loan management process can give loan officers an advantage in accomplishing those tasks. □

Break-Even Analysis

Break-Even Analysis and Operating Leverage

by Dev Strischek

If a borrower cannot break even, he probably cannot repay his loan. In the following article, Dev Strischek describes a short-cut approach to finding the break-even sales point by dividing the gross profit margin into all the fixed costs. He also presents a short-cut method for calculating operating leverage and explains how the operating leverage ratio can provide a clue to sales-profit sensitivity.

The author is senior vice president, credit services, Barnett Bank of Palm Beach County, Palm Beach, Florida. At the time this article was originally published in October 1983, he was senior vice president, Barnett Bank of South Florida, Miami.

The recessions we have suffered over the past ten years have forced us to focus our attention on how much our commercial borrowers depend on sales stability, real sales growth, and adequate profit margins to repay their debts. Volatile sales may not always cover overhead, and price increases that lag behind rising expenses mean that cost-push inflation will negate the additional profits. The successful firm sets prices that simultaneously attract enough demand and yield enough margin to cover all costs and generate the desired income.

The purpose of this article is to examine two closely linked techniques that can provide commercial bankers with answers to two basic questions:

1. What level of sales is necessary to break even?
2. How sensitive are profits to changes in sales?

A banker should know how much his borrower must sell to cover all his costs and how much profits will change when sales rise or fall. Both questions are crucial to estimating the time and profitability of repayment.

Break-even analysis

Break-even analysis is undertaken to determine what sales level will allow a firm to cover all its costs. The banker's principal use of this technique is to compare actual cumulative sales to the break-even point to determine if and when his borrower will be earning a profit and generating funds for loan repayment.

Variable and fixed costs

Break-even sales occur at that point where revenues cover all costs. Costs are classified into two groups, variable costs and fixed costs. By definition, sales cause variable costs, so variable costs change as sales change. If there were no sales, there would be no variable costs. Examples of variable costs include sales commissions, direct labor, raw materials, and freight and shipping.

Important to later discussion in this article, cost of goods sold tends to behave as a variable cost because most of its components are usually classified as variable costs. Expenses for such components as direct labor and materials would not be incurred if there were no sales.

In contrast, fixed costs do not vary with sales. Even if there were no sales, these costs would still be incurred. Examples of fixed costs include officers' salaries, rent and lease expense, general and administrative expenses, utilities expenses, and property taxes and licenses.

Many of the so-called operating expenses are essentially fixed costs because they would have to be paid regardless of the sales level.

Differentiating between fixed and variable costs is usually the hardest step in break-even analysis. However, a short-cut method that lumps together all the "hard-to-classify" expenses as fixed costs will be shown later to result in a good but conservative banker's approximation of the break-even point.

Calculation of the break-even point

The break-even point can be calculated graphically or algebraically. We will discuss the graphic approach first because it illustrates some basic points about break-even analysis. The data for both our proofs will be derived from income and expense data for the Breakfast Corporation portrayed in Figure 1.

Figure 1—Income and Expense Data of the Breakfast Corporation for the Year Ended 12/31/81

Income Statement	$M	% of Sales
Sales	3,600	100.0
Cost of Goods Sold	2,700	75.0
Gross Profit	900	25.0
Operating Expenses	435	12.1
Earnings before Interest and Taxes	465	12.9
Interest Expense	15	.4
Profit before Taxes	450	12.5

	Costs ($M)		
Expenses	Fixed	Variable	Total
Materials		1,800	1,800
Labor		900	900
Commissions		100	100
General and Administrative	145		145
Depreciation	40		40
Interest	15		15
Rent	150		150
Total	350	2,800	3,150

The concept underlying the graphic approach is that break even occurs where sales equal costs. So the two axes of the graph in Figure 2 have equivalent scales. We assign sales to the horizontal axis and costs to the vertical axis because dependent variables are customarily assigned to the vertical axis. We are assuming that some of our costs' existence depends on the making of sales.

Our first step is to graph the fixed costs. Figure 1 indicates that they total some $350,000. The horizontal line extending from the 350 mark on the vertical "cost" axis of Figure 2 implies that regardless of the sales level, Breakfast Corporation must spend annually $350,000 in fixed costs.

Our second step is to graph the variable costs. By definition, these costs vary in direct proportion to sales, and Figure 1's data indicate that variable costs totaled $2.8 million on sales of $3.6 million. Thus, variable costs amounted to $78 of every $100 of sales. We overlay the variable cost wedge on top of the fixed costs' horizontal line to arrive at a total cost line which when intersected by a break-even sales-costs line will give us the break-even point.

At zero sales, we have no variable costs, but at $100,000, we would have $78,000, which is shown in Figure 2 as point A. Likewise, the $200,000 sales

Figure 2—Break-Even Graph

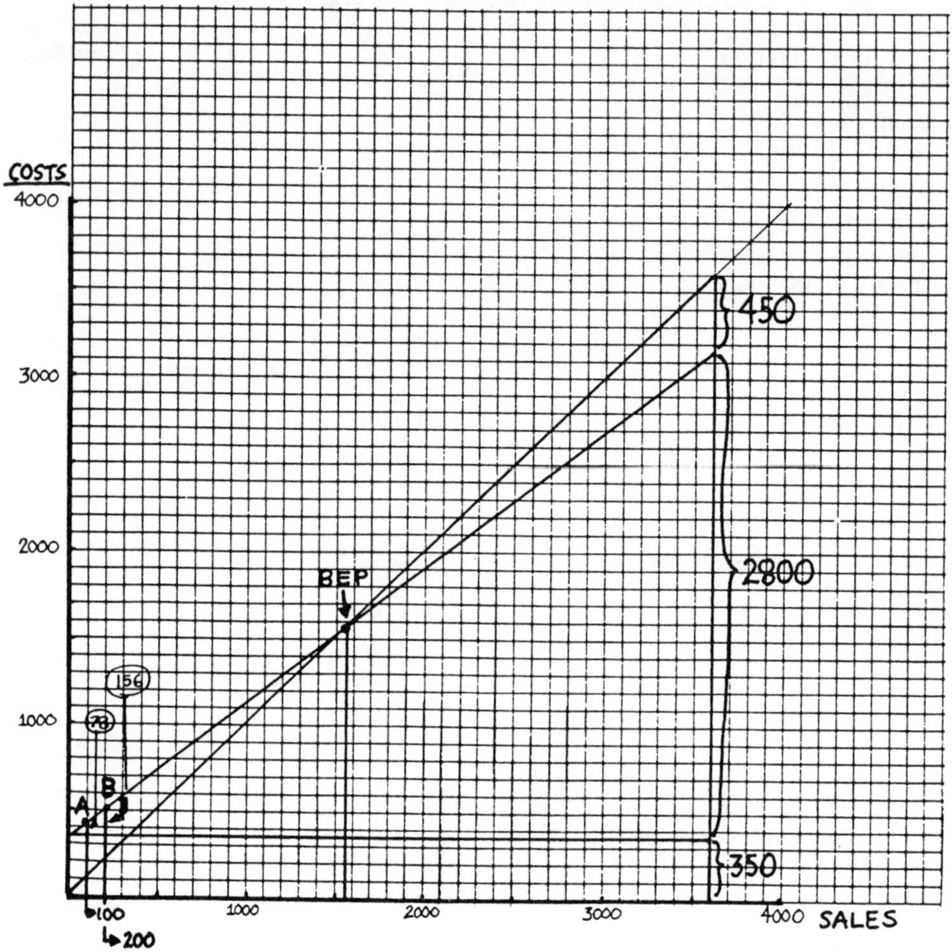

level would require $156,000 of variable costs and is identified as point B. Another way of describing points A and B is that at the $100,000 level, total costs equal $428,000 ($350,000 of fixed costs plus $78,000 of variable costs) and that at the $200,000 level, total costs equal $506,000 ($350,000 of fixed costs plus $156,000 of variable costs). By connecting points A and B, we can construct a total costs line.

Our final step is to draw in the break-even sales line. This break-even line will always be equidistant from both the vertical and horizontal axes because along the break-even line, costs must equal sales. Where this line intersects our total cost line, we will have our break-even sales point. By dropping a line down to the horizontal axis, we can determine break-even sales. Casual observation of Figure 2 suggests that the break-even sales point is about \$1.6 million. At that level, \$1.25 million of variable costs are incurred, leaving \$350,000 of margin to be contributed toward covering the \$350,000 of fixed costs.

The graphic approach is visually rewarding as an illustration of the break-even concept, but it is too imprecise and too time-consuming to be useful in timely, accurate problem-solving. A formula would serve us better, and if we retrace the steps we took in the graphic solution, we can derive an equation for estimating the break-even sales point.

First, let us consider the role played by profit margins. We incur variable costs any time that we make sales, so we assume that we must first pay our variable costs. The remainder is then available to cover fixed costs. We call this difference the "contribution" because it represents the revenues remaining after paying variable costs that can be contributed to covering the fixed costs.

We can express the contribution as a percent of sales because it is usually a stable relationship. This contribution margin can then be applied to a sales figure to yield the amount available to cover fixed costs. The following proof outlines the derivation of the break-even formula:

$$\text{break-even sales (BES)} = \text{variable costs (VC)} + \text{fixed costs (FC)}$$

$$BES = VC + FC$$

$$S - VC = FC$$

$$S - VC = \text{contribution to covering fixed costs}$$

$$\frac{S - VC}{S} = \text{CM, contribution margin as a \% of sales}$$

$$\frac{S - VC}{S} = \frac{FC}{S}$$

$$CM = \frac{FC}{S}$$

$$BES = \frac{FC}{CM}$$

Thus, break-even sales can be calculated by dividing the contribution margin into fixed costs.

Breakfast Corporation's \$1.6 million graphic solution is substantiated by the formula's solution of \$1,576,576 as shown at the top of page 134.

$$\text{BES} = \frac{\text{FC}}{\text{CM}}$$

$$= \frac{350{,}000}{(800{,}000/3{,}600{,}000)} = \frac{350{,}000}{22.2\%}$$

$$= \frac{350{,}000}{.222} = \underline{\underline{1{,}576{,}576}}$$

Simplifications

The contribution margin bears a canny resemblance to gross profit margin (GPM), and for just a small trade-off in precision, there is much to be gained by a short-cut method substituting gross proft margin for contribution margin.

The first advantage is simplification of the break-even concept. Calculating the break-even point of any business becomes a simple matter of dividing the firm's fixed costs by its GPM.

The second advantage of this short-cut approach is that the break-even point calculated is a little higher than under the more precise method of carefully isolating variable costs from fixed costs. Figure 1 indicates that Breakfast Corporation's gross profit was $900,000 versus a contribution of $800,000. The $100,000 difference is the sales commission expense which is classified as a fixed cost under the short-cut method so that the gross profit margin can be used as the contribution margin. The result is that the short-cut method yields a higher and more conservative break-even point of $1,800,000 than the precise method's $1,576,000:

Calculation of Break-Even Sales ($M)	Method: Precise		Method: Short-Cut	
Sales	3,600		3,600	
VC	2,800		2,700	
Contribution	800		900	
Contribution/Sales = CM	800/3,600	= 22.2%	900/3,600	= 25.0%
FC	350		450	
FC/CM = BES	1,576		1,800	

What we have accomplished so far is how to graphically or algebraically calculate the break-even sales point. We can approximate the BES point by dividing the gross profit margin into the rest of a company's expenses, which are assumed to be fixed. The short-cut method gives us bankers a margin for error to protect us from our borrowers' optimistic sales projections as well as a simple formula for calculating the break-even point.

Goals and the break-even point

The lower the break-even point, the lower the sales level needed to generate a profit. Lowering the break-even point is a function of three alternatives:

1. Increasing the selling price per unit
2. Reducing the variable cost per unit
3. Reducing fixed costs

However, these simple alternatives are not so simple to apply, and where the contribution margin is very narrow, much more revenue is required to cover fixed costs. For example, if Breakfast Corporation's gross profit margin slipped from 25% to 10%, it would have to increase sales by a 2.5 multiple from $1.8 million to $4.5 million to cover its $450,000 of fixed costs. In effect, the contribution margin exerts a sort of inverse leverage on sales, so the lower the contribution margin is, the higher the break-even sales required. Moreover, if fixed costs rise, each incremental increase in these costs requires additional sales at some multiple of the fixed costs. One way of calculating this multiple is to measure what impact a change in sales has on profits. This multiple is sometimes called the operating leverage.

Operating leverage

Operating leverage compares the gross profit earned on sales to the fixed costs, and we define operating leverage as the contribution available to cover fixed costs in relation to operating income. In "short-cut" terms, we can approximate operating leverage by dividing before-tax profits into the gross profit:

$$\text{Operating leverage} = \frac{\text{contribution to fixed costs}}{\text{operating income}}$$

$$= \frac{\text{sales - variable costs}}{\text{sales - variable costs - fixed costs}}$$

$$= \frac{\text{gross profit}}{\text{profit before taxes}} = \frac{\text{GP}}{\text{PBT}}$$

The operating leverage (OL) ratio will tell us how much each 1% change in sales will change operating income. If the ratio is 2.0, then a 10% increase in sales will result in a 20% increase in before-tax profits. A 10% drop in sales will cut before-tax profits by 20%.

Operating leverage ratio

Indeed, Breakfast Corporation's operating leverage is 2.0, and 10% changes in sales does result in 20% changes in profits:

Breakfast Corporation Income Statement ($M)	**1981**	**Change in Sales +10%**	**−10%**
Sales	3,600	3,960	3,240
COGS	2,700	2,970	2,430
GP	900	990	810
−FC	450	450	450
PBT	450	540	360
% INCR (DECR) PBT	—	20%	(20%)
OL = GP/PBT	2.0X	—	—

Used in this context, the operating leverage ratio gives us some measure of the sensitivity of the bottom-line to changes in sales. It follows that risk-averse bankers should be wary of borrowers and industries with high operating leverage and volatile sales.

Industry data

Industry statistics suggest that operating leverage tends to increase as products move through the distribution channel from manufacturers through wholesalers to retailers. For example, the 1981-82 women's clothing operating leverage ratios rise from a manufacturer's 6.0 through the wholesaler's 9.0 to the retailer's 16.2, according to Figure 3. Thus, a 10% drop in sales would mean a 60% drop in before-tax profits at the women's clothing manufacturing level, a 90% decline at the wholesale level, and a 102% fall at the retail level.

The higher operating leverages at the retail level suggest that retailers have higher fixed costs and inherent riskier situations that justify their generally fatter gross profit margins. Retailers are also at the end of the distribution channel and more directly exposed to shifts in ultimate consumer demand.

The three years of data in Figure 3 also reflect the volatility of the operating leverage ratios. The ratios change from year to year in response to changing conditions in the economy and the industry. Although operating leverage still tends to increase as goods flow from the manufacturing to the retail level, bankers must also be cognizant of the business cycle stage and the industry's condition.

Figure 3—Operating Leverage by Level of Distribution

Industry		as % of Sales						Operating Leverage (GP/PBT)		
		1979-80		1980-81		1981-82				
SIC	Name	GP	PBT	GP	PBT	GP	PBT	1979-80	1980-81	1981-82
2335	mfr, women's clothing	28.3	4.1	26.8	2.9	28.3	4.7	6.9	9.2	6.0
5137	whl, women's clothing	28.5	3.1	25.5	2.5	25.2	2.8	9.2	10.2	9.0
5621	ret, women's clothing	40.8	2.7	40.9	2.6	40.5	2.5	15.1	15.7	16.2
2512	mfr, furniture	23.1	3.4	23.6	3.8	23.1	2.8	6.8	6.2	8.2
5021	whl, furniture	28.0	3.7	29.4	3.1	29.2	2.2	7.6	9.5	13.3
5712	ret, furniture	39.9	4.0	40.2	2.7	39.2	1.6	10.0	14.9	24.5
2084-5	mfr, wine & liquor	21.6	4.5	23.9	4.3	21.6	3.0	4.8	5.6	7.2
5182	whl, wine & liquor	21.1	3.0	21.2	2.7	21.8	2.7	7.0	7.8	8.1
5921	ret, wine & liquor	20.6	2.5	20.5	1.6	21.4	3.4	8.2	12.8	6.3
3143	mfr, shoes	22.5	3.2	24.4	5.5	25.6	5.6	7.0	4.4	4.6
5139	whl, shoes	23.7	2.8	24.4	1.1	26.8	4.2	8.5	22.2	6.4
5661	ret, shoes	41.8	4.4	42.4	3.6	41.3	2.9	9.5	11.8	14.2

Source: *1982 Annual Statement Studies* (Philadelphia: Robert Morris Associates, 1982). Statistics are drawn from comparative historical data columns.

Break-even sales and operating leverage

The formula below shows the relationship between a firm's annual sales and its break-even sales point. Breakfast Corporation's operating leverage of 2.0 means it breaks even at 50% of its annual sales:

$$\text{Break-even Sales} = \underline{(\text{OL} - 1)}\ (\text{Annual Sales})$$

$$= \frac{(2 - 1)}{(\ 2\ )}\ \text{Annual Sales}$$

$$= 50\% \times \text{Annual Sales} = .50 \times 3{,}600{,}000 = 1{,}800{,}000$$

If its operating leverage ratio had been 4, 75% of Breakfast's annual sales would be required just to break even. At a ratio of 10, 90% of sales would be required to break even. If Breakfast Corporation's year-end is December 31, and 6-month sales are $1.8 million, the banker can probably feel reasonably comfortable that Breakfast will have a profitable year with a 2.0 operating leverage. That comfort level would be considerably less at the end of June if Breakfast had a 10.0 operating leverage and needed 90% of annual sales to break even. Obviously, the higher the operating leverage, the higher the sales level required to break even.

Summary

Break-even analysis can tell the banker what sales level his borrower must achieve to cover all his costs. A short-cut approach to finding the break-even sales point is to divide the gross profit margin into all the operating expenses. The result usually has a safety margin on the high side to protect the banker against the borrower's optimistically low break-even sales points.

Operating leverage provides a clue to sales-profit sensitivity. Dividing the gross profit by the before-tax profit yields a ratio that tells by how much a given change in sales will be magnified and carried to the bottom line. Higher operating leverage means bigger swings in profits as sales vary. Operating leverage appears to increase as goods flow from manufacturers through wholesalers to retailers. Thus, the risk of profit downswings in recessions seems to increase as goods move to the ultimate consumer.

As operating leverage declines, so will the break-even point. Lower operating leverage occurs when the gross profit margin increases as a result of higher unit selling prices, lower unit costs, or lower fixed costs. Rising operating leverage means potentially greater profit volatility and higher break-even sales levels, so appraising the borrower's credit risk may be improved if its break-even point and operating leverage are monitored periodically. □

More on Break-Even Analysis

by Venkatesan Srinivasan

In an article published in the Journal *in October 1983 and included in this collection, Dev Strischek demonstrated the usefulness of break-even analysis in assessing the performance of a firm and its repayment capability. The concept can be extended to compute break-even points in terms of the firm's cash flows as well as to derive a measure for the margin of safety that is available to the banker at the firm's current operating levels.*

The author is assistant professor, College of Business Administration, Northeastern University, Boston, Massachusetts. At the time this article was originally published in July 1984, he was a doctoral student at the University of Cincinnati, Ohio.

In assessing a firm's repayment capability, banks have increasingly turned their attention to the relative stability of an enterprise. Volatile economic conditions have led banks to focus attention on the ability of a firm to generate a steady level of sales and maintain its profit margins despite adversities. In his article entitled, "Break-even Analysis and Operating Leverage," that appeared in the October 1983 issue of the *Journal*, Dev Strischek discussed the usefulness of the conventional break-even analysis to the bank lender and linked it to the sensitivity of a firm's profits given a change in sales. The following questions were examined in that article:

1. What level of sales is necessary to break even?
2. How sensitive are profits to changes in sales?

The above questions are of prime concern to the banker. They shed light on the viability of the prospective loan or the repayment capacity of the borrower, as the case may be. Strischek's analysis, however, presented the break-even in terms of the firm's accounting profits. It is reasonable to expect that the banker would be more interested in the cash flows generated by the firm, and the analysis can be extended to compute the break-even in terms of cash flows. However, I think it would be helpful also to highlight the usefulness of a measure to examine the margin of safety that the current operating level provides. I will try to do that in this article by examining the following questions:

1. What level of sales is necessary to break even in terms of cash flows?
2. Based on current operating levels, what is the margin of safety?

Break-even analysis

It is useful to recapitulate briefly some of the concepts underlying break-even analysis. Break-even sales are defined as the level of sales that enables the firm to meet all its costs and leaves no profit or loss. Costs are grouped as variable or fixed costs. Conventionally, there is a third category consisting of costs that are partially variable. But as Strischek pointed out in his earlier article, a short-cut method to avoid practical difficulties of categorizing costs is to regard the cost of goods as variable with sales and to lump together the rest of the expenses as fixed costs.

Bias in considering costs as variable or fixed

Obviously, expenses lumped together in this manner yield a somewhat biased result. This can be viewed as a conservative approach to the analysis since the direction of the bias in this case would result in a more conservative estimate of the break-even point. However, analysts should also be aware that assuming that cost of goods sold is perfectly variable yields a bias in the opposite direction. Cost of goods sold embodies certain allocated overhead costs and labor in addition to material costs. To the extent some of the allocated overhead costs are fixed, such an assumption would result in lowering the break-even point computed. In cases where the allocated overhead costs (fixed) form a material percentage of the cost of goods sold, it might be worthwhile to adjust for this bias even though this would require additional effort and time.

Formulas for computing break-even sales

Figure 1 details the income and expense statement of the Breakfast Corporation for the year ended December 31, 1981. This example is almost the same as that used by Strischek. Let us also summarize the relationships highlighted by Strischek:

1. Break-even Sales (BES) = Variable Costs (VC) + Fixed Costs (FC)
2. Contribution Margin Ratio* (CM) = (Sales − Variable Costs)/Sales
3. Using 1 and 2 above, BES = FC/CM

* For the break-even point, this may also be defined as fixed costs/sales.

Figure 1—Income and Expense Data of the Breakfast Corporation for the Year Ended December 31, 1981

Income Statement:	$M	% of Sales*
Sales	3,600	100.00
Cost of Goods Sold	2,800	77.80
Gross Profit	800	22.20
Operating Expenses	435	12.08
Earnings before Interest and Taxes	365	10.12
Interest	15	0.42
Profit before Taxes	350	9.70

	Costs ($M)		
Expenses:	Fixed	Variable	Total
Materials		1,800	1,800
Labor		1,000	1,000
Commissions		—	—
General and Administrative	245		245
Depreciation	40		40
Interest	15		15
Rent	150		150
Total	450	2,800	3,250

As stated earlier, for practical considerations, cost of goods sold can be considered as variable and operating costs as fixed. By subtracting the variable costs from sales revenue, we obtain the contribution margin. It is important to note that by definition, therefore, this margin will be relatively stable. It is obvious that if the firm generates enough contribution margin to cover its fixed costs, it will break even. Since by definition, a unit change in sales will result in a uniform change in the contribution margin (change = CM times change in sales), break-even sales may be found using the third formula given at the bottom of the previous page.

Extensions

The break-even analysis briefly illustrated above can be extended to yield more analytical insight. Using the third formula above yields break-even in terms of sales dollars. Break-even points can be computed in terms of number of units that the firm needs to sell. To do so, we need to know the per unit variable cost and selling price. This may not be difficult to obtain, particularly if the company has a good system of costing and control. The formula is as follows:

$$\text{BES (in number of units)} = \text{FC/CM per unit (\$)}$$

Let us make a simplifying assumption that the Breakfast Corporation sells only one type of product and that the following information is available:

Selling price	= \$3.60 per unit
Variable costs	= \$2.80 per unit

Break-even sales in units is computed as follows:

$$\text{BES (in units)} = \frac{\text{FC}}{\text{CM/unit}} = \frac{450}{0.80} = 562.5 \text{ or } 563 \text{ units}$$

One of the limitations of break-even analysis is that the results obtained on a firm's aggregate income and expense statement can be misleading in the case where the firm sells a number of products. Thus computing the BES in units would depend on the availability of information to break down the aggregate data by products.

Reformulating BES for cash flow break-even

The second extension is in reformulating the accounting BES as computed by Strischek to a cash flow break-even. From a banker's perspective, cash flows would appear to be more important than the company's net income or operating profit, as the case may be. We are measuring the firm's ability to repay the loan's principal and interest, so the level of cash flows bears directly on the issue. The cash flow break-even measures the relationship between total sales revenues and cash flows. For the Breakfast Corporation, we would exclude depreciation from the computations to arrive at the cash flow break-even:

Cash flow break-even:

	$	%	$/unit
Sales	3,600	100.00	3.60
Variable Costs	2,800	77.80	2.80
Contribution Margin	800	22.20	0.80
Fixed Costs (Excluding Depreciation)	410		$410
BES (cash flow)	1,847		513 units
BES (in accounting profits)	2,027		563 units

Figure 2—Margin of Safety

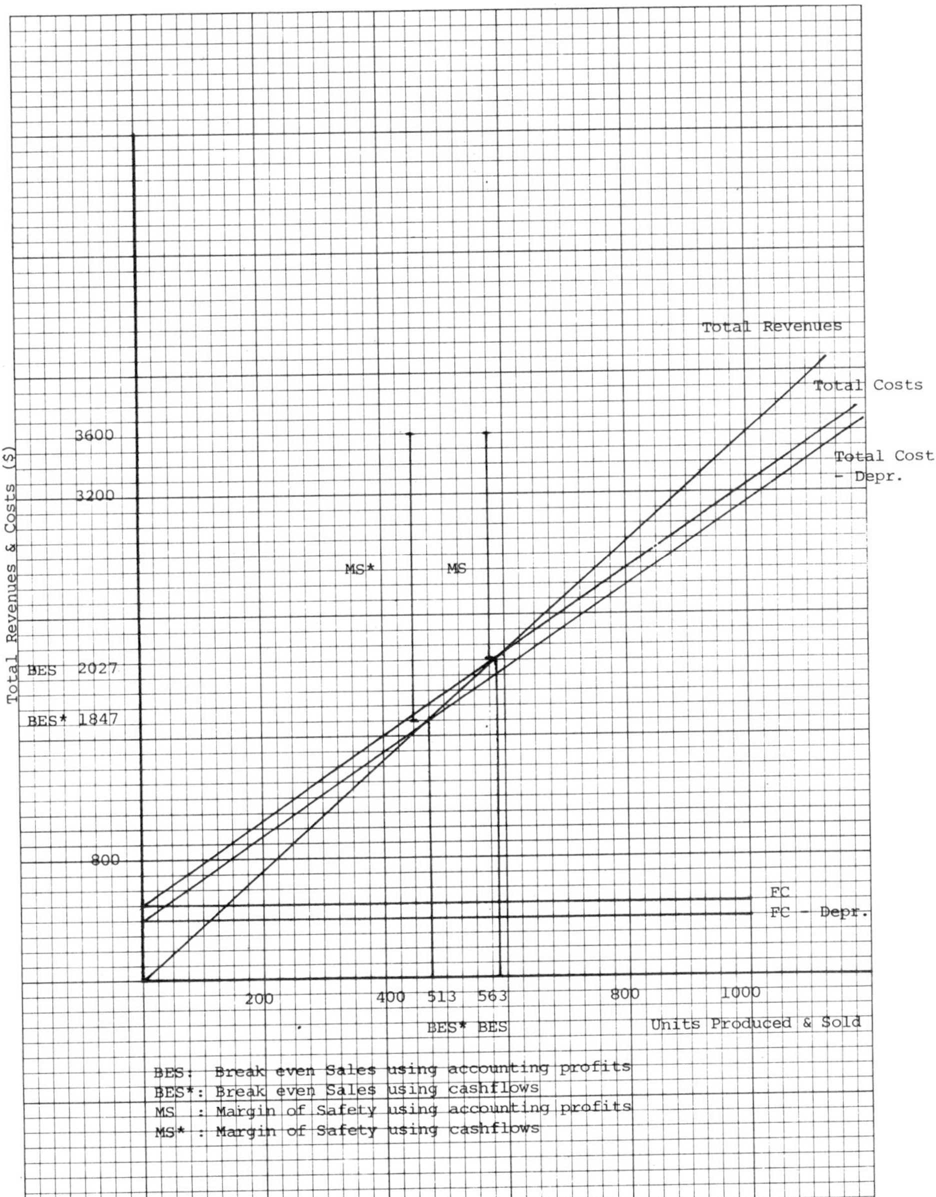

We can observe that the cash flow break-even is somewhat lower than the accounting break-even because of the exclusion of noncash charges. Figure 2 illustrates the cash flow BES graphically.

Margin of safety

Finally, the analysis can be extended to derive a margin-of-safety measure based on current operating levels and the break-even sales. Margin of safety in this context can be defined as the margin by which the current operations are above the break-even point. Any drop in operating volume below this margin will result in an insufficient coverage for fixed costs:

$$\text{Margin of Safety (MS)} = \frac{\text{Current Sales} - \text{Break-even Sales}}{\text{Current Sales}}$$

$$'' \quad (\%) = \text{MS} \times 100.$$

In the case of Breakfast Corporation, we can compute the margin of safety using both the break-even sales in terms of accounting profits as well as cash flows.

Let us denote the BES in terms of accounting profits as BES and the cash flow BES as BES* for distinction.

Margin of Safety:

$$\text{MS (using BES)} = \frac{3{,}600 - 2{,}027}{3{,}600} = .4369 \text{ or } 43.69\%$$

$$\text{MS (using BES*)} = \frac{3{,}600 - 1{,}847}{3{,}600} = .4869 \text{ or } 48.69\%$$

The margin can also be illustrated graphically as shown in Figure 2. Combined with operating leverage, the margin of safety can enable the banker to assess the degree of risk involved by lending to a prospective buyer or the committed risk in the case of an existing borrower.

Summary

Notwithstanding the various limitations that are expressed against break-even analyses, it remains an easy-to-use, intuitively appealing tool to an analyst. The methods suggested above are somewhat simplistic and are short-cut approaches. However, the banker will be able to estimate the firm's operating capability and the borrower's probable degree of default risk. The analysis can also aid the banker in detecting overly optimistic forecasts and thus represents a quick decision tool that does not require too much time or effort. □

Author's update

There are two important extensions to the analysis presented in my original article: incorporating uncertainty and incorporating advances in computer and information technologies for credit analysis.

Incorporating uncertainty

My analysis here assumes that sales and cost of goods sold are known with certainty. While sensitivity analysis can be conducted by varying sales and cost of goods sold, the analysis can be enhanced to reflect uncertainty explicitly in one of two ways: probabilistic estimates and Monte Carlo simulation. Probabilistic analysis is useful in cases where the credit analyst can estimate subjective probabilities for sales and cost of goods sold.

To illustrate, consider the example presented in the previous section. Suppose the credit analyst were not confident that the firm will actually achieve $3,600 in sales but has the following subjective estimates:

% Chance	Sales	Cost of Goods Sold
20%	$3,100	70% of sales
30	$3,600	75% of sales
30	$3,700	77% of sales
20	$4,000	80% of sales

This table indicates the credit analyst's subjective estimate that there is a 20% chance the firm will actually have sales of only $3,100, with a 70% cost-of-goods-sold-to-sales ratio and so on. Given such estimates, useful insight into the average expected sales can be obtained by computing a weighted average of the above estimates (mean). The credit analyst can also get an idea of the possible deviations from the average by computing the standard deviation or the coefficient of variation.

Formulas for computing standard deviation or the coefficient of variation can be found in any introductory statistics text. Break-even analysis can be conducted by considering the mean level of sales while keeping in view the possible deviations indicated by the standard deviation.

On the other hand, suppose the best that the credit analyst can do is determine that the sales of the company can be anywhere between $2,500 and $3,600 and that the cost of goods sold can be between 65% and 80%. One approach to take in such cases is to conduct extensive sensitivity analysis. But since the number of potential sales/cost-of-goods-sold combinations is very large, this can be quite tedious. A feasible approach in such cases is to do Monte Carlo simulation.

This is done by repeatedly choosing a random level of sales in the $2,500–$3,600 interval and correspondingly choosing a random cost-of-goods-sold percentage in the 65–80% interval and conducting break-even analysis. This analysis is repeated a large number of times, each time choosing a new random sales and cost-of-goods-sold estimates. The credit analyst can profile the potential outcome by plotting the results of each iteration of the simulation. An average can be computed over the results of the iterations, and, as before, an idea of possible deviation from such an average can be obtained by computing the standard deviation.

Incorporating advances in computer technology

Implementation of the break-even analysis models presented in the original article can be easily done using a spread sheet package like Lotus 1-2-3. However, more frequently, break-even analysis is just one part of the credit investigation that a credit analyst undertakes. Different models and information are required for such analysis.

Due to the tremendous advances in computer and information technologies, it is possible to design and develop support systems that enable the analyst to integrate these models and significantly enhance his or her analytical capabilities. Adaptation of such advances to aid decision making initially resulted in two classes of systems: decision support systems and expert systems. However, as research and practice in developing such systems have evolved, it is increasingly being recognized that a particular decision process such as credit analysis can be supported by a combination of decision support and expert systems.

This is now leading to the development of expert support systems. The idea here is that the more structured aspects of a decision process can be supported by expert subsystems and the more unstructured aspects of the process can be supported by decision support subsystems. While this discussion is only superficial and brief, the author has conducted extensive research on designing and developing such systems with the partial support of the Credit Research Foundation, and the results are available from the author. □

ORDER FORM

RMA'S SPECIAL COLLECTIONS FROM THE *JOURNAL*

Price: $28 **Discount Price for RMA member institutions: $22**

Loan Review	______ copies	$ ________ 36010
Spilled Milk, Vol. 1	______ copies	$ ________ 36011
Spilled Milk, Vol. 2	______ copies	$ ________ 36036
Real Estate and Construction Lending	______ copies	$ ________ 36014
Problem Loans	______ copies	$ ________ 36015
Risk Management	______ copies	$ ________ 36022
Credit Analysis	______ copies	$ ________ 36026
Small Business Financing	______ copies	$ ________ 36027
Developing a Basic Loan Training Program, 2nd Ed.	______ copies	$ ________ 36028
Bankruptcy	______ copies	$ ________ 36033
Lender Liability	______ copies	$ ________ 36034
Asset-Based Lending	______ copies	$ ________ 36035
	Pa. residents, add 6% sales tax	$ ________
	TOTAL	$ ________

Name ____

Function ____

Institution ____

Address ____

City ____________________ State ______________ Zip ________

Phone ____________________ Asset Size $ ______________

All orders must be accompanied by payment. Please allow 4-6 weeks for delivery. Prices subject to change without notice. All payments must be made in U.S. dollars, and all checks must be drawn on U.S. banks. Send this order form with your payment to Order Department, Robert Morris Associates, P.O. Box 8500 S-1140, Philadelphia, PA 19178 (215) 665-2850.

CAB/BA

1.5M 11/86

1M 7/87

2M 5/88